THE REBELLIOUS RECOVERY

THE
REBELLIOUS
RECOVERY

TRANSFORM YOUR ADVERSITY INTO ADVENTURE

A MEMOIR BY
AARON BAKER

PNEUMIND
LOS ANGELES. CA

Published by PNEUMIND
contact@therebelliousrecovery.com

PNEUMIND books are available at special quantity discounts for bulk purchase for sales promotions, premiums, fundraising, and educational needs. Special books or book excerpts also can be created to fit specific needs. For details and permission requests, write to the email address above.

ISBN 979-8-9864880-1-1 (hardback)
ISBN 979-8-9864880-0-4 (paperback)
ISBN 979-8-9864880-2-8 (eBook)

www.therebelliousrecovery.com

www.imaaronbaker.com

Printed in the United States of America

—

Content Editor: Stephanie Mojica
Copy Editor: James Gallagher
Cover Designer: Adam Bice
Cover Photo: Chris Boulton
Publisher & Book Designer: Kory Kirby
SET IN CRIMSON TEXT

rebellious

....

/rə-ˈbel-yəs/

adjective

1. showing a desire to resist authority, control, or convention.
2. (of a person, city, or state) engaged in opposition or resistance to an established government or ruler.
3. (of a thing) not easily handled or kept in place.

recovery

....

/rə-ˈkə-v(ə)-rē/

noun

1. a return to a normal state of health, mind, or strength.
2. the action or process of regaining possession or control of something stolen or lost.

"Strength does not come from physical capacity.
It comes from an indomitable will."
—MAHATMA GANDHI

CONTENTS

CONTENTS

PART 6: SERVE & SHARE

FOREWORD

"The past is done. The future is unwritten. Take care of now."

I first met Aaron Baker early on in his journey from teenage moto-cross athlete to spinal-cord-injury insurgent. He was training at an adaptive gym with a man-on-a-mission intensity, hoping to awaken his broken body. This was indeed an act of rebellion—a challenge to the prevailing belief that there was nothing anybody could do about recovering from a paralyzing injury.

Aaron's first response was like everybody's—retreat into denial, spiral into depression. He was scared, angry, helpless, and not far from cashing himself out. But Aaron backed away from the edge of that pool. He thought, *Wait a minute. This is not the script I was handed, but I'm not letting this define me. I'm going to reinvent myself and write my own pages with the same full-throttle passion I had as a pro dirt-bike rider.*

The Rebellious Recovery is the tale of a young man on a quest for adventure, friendship, love, and family. The book presents the full California-raised sunbaked character—well traveled, confident, and enthralled by girls, surfing, motorsports, and speed.

All was just swell, until one day it wasn't, and Aaron had to face a new reality, a new body, a new world to figure out. Immobility. Loss of independence. Bladder and bowel set on auto-accidental. But also hints of recovery and a first hug with Mom. Then eventually a revelation, a new mind, and a new mission.

This is much more than a biography. It's a philosophy of life. Aaron's recovery has become his life work—an inspiration to those whose lives have gone off the rails. Within these pages, Aaron shares strategies for turning a lousy prognosis into a vital life force.

The Rebellious Recovery flips the script on misery and boils it down to this: obstacles are opportunities. We need to recognize what we can control and what we cannot. What's essential is not what happened—it's about your response to it.

Make peace with the face in your mirror, resist the headwinds of self-doubt, and decide to go forward. *Keep it simple*, says Aaron. Focus on the things you can do something about. Move through adversity by making good choices with your body and well-being. Be resourceful, be kind, be grateful. See things as they are, not as the way you always thought they were going to be.

Adversity is the adventure, says Aaron, and to fully embrace this, you may have to be a bit of a rebel. Don't wait. You don't need to ask anyone's permission. Go for it!

—SAM MADDOX, JOURNALIST & AUTHOR
LOS ANGELES, CALIFORNIA, 2022

PREFACE

*"My achievements do little to contribute to the world unless they
illustrate something fundamental about me and about you."*

My intention for writing this memoir is more than just to share por-
tions of my life with you. I want my history to inspire and provoke
you to think of your own story as an adventure and for the construct
of these pages to become a mirror for your mind, a portal to travel
forward and back and expand exponentially.

What I realized while writing is that a recurring motif manifested itself—one of simplicity. In most aspects of my adult journey
I found myself reverting back to simple thoughts, the **B.A.S.I.C.S**
of my mind. I see this as my blueprint, the framework from which
I built and rebuilt, defined and redefined my life, time and again. I
seemed to have assembled the pieces of myself in a simple step-by-step
process—a cyclical pattern of six parts—a road map: the beginning,
my self-awareness, a vulnerable surrender, inspiration, a deep commitment, and a passion for sharing. These fundamentals have led me
to experience true self-improvement and extraordinary achievement
in the face of adversity.

In the context of this memoir, the **Beginning** represents my early
life history, the proverbial seeds of curiosity and openness that were
planted in me as a boy. My **Self-Awareness** came in the form of trauma,
a profound experience that amplified my sensitivity and consciousness.

The moment I **Surrendered** to my pain and allowed the darkness to be seen as an essential epoch of experience, an immense transformation occurred. I found the bottom—a sturdy place to build upon. **Inspiration** takes many forms—little sparks of hope that I kindled—the flame of which, through **Commitment** over spans of time, was fanned into a fire—the underpinning secret to most of my success. In the end, my purpose was revealed through the process—to **Serve and Share** my journey, my time, and my love.

HASHTAGS

Own your adversity. Share your adventure. Use these hashtags. I'm excited to follow along!

#therebelliousrecovery

#myrebelliousstory

#backtothebasics

#thebasicsmethod

#adversityistheadventure

#paintedtoes

INTRODUCTION

Felo-de-se (Medieval Latin): "A felon of himself"

I was alone, no kids splashing, families barbecuing, or sunbathers in sight as my wheels bumped over the cracks in the concrete—I slowly rounded the edge of the swimming pool.

We'd been at it for almost a year when Toots decided she needed a break from the routine to drive back to Oklahoma to pick up the rest of her belongings. Left home alone with my darkening thoughts, I found myself unable to bear the wheelchair any longer and became desperate to take matters into my own hands.

The sun was setting behind me, warming my neck as the heat radiated off the light-gray deck. With the joystick delicately resting between my left thumb and index finger, I maneuvered my electric-powered wheelchair to the lipped edge at the deep end of the pool, my front wheels less than an inch from the water.

Eight feet was an abyss for my two-hundred-pound chair. I gazed deep into the glassy water, my tear-stained reflection staring back. I realized there was no difference between the watery depth I stared into and the darkness of my mind. I was tired, exhausted from fighting my mind and body, unable to make the same connection to life as I'd always done, with no future in mind except the burden I had become.

Gravity was crushing me. As ambiguous, muffled sounds of nature and everyday life played out all around me, I sat quietly. It would be easy. One jolt of my joystick forward would send me into oblivion, a familiar end of life . . . just like my death experience one year before.

My mind was black.

PROLOGUE

"I like to muse that life happens for us, not to us."

Still As Stone

A warm, subtle glow crept upon my cheek as I stretched and yawned beneath a mustard-yellow goose-down duvet cover adorned with a stitched geometric pattern and tiny gray elephants. The early-morning sun winked through the window at the head of my bed and invited me to get up and out into the world.

Certain details about that Memorial Day weekend in 1999 flash in my mind like freeze-frames, played and replayed over and over.

I was a new houseguest living with the owner of the professional race team I had been a part of for five months. He and his family had graciously invited me to stay with them in their two-story suburban tract home in a small town called Simi Valley, about thirty miles northwest of Los Angeles.

I log-rolled over to the right side of the bed and out from under the blanket. My bare feet were on the new-smelling beige carpet, and I curled my toes into the weave, stretching and yawning again. I reached under the bed to dig through a disheveled pile of semiclean oversize teenage clothes that smelled more like pheromones than laundry detergent. I selected my bright-blue skateboard shoes and my favorite red baseball hat, then stuffed my chain wallet into my back pocket. I hastily left the room and blitzed down the two flights of carpeted stairs, touching down only twice as I grabbed my skateboard at the bottom and burst into the garage, excited to ride my new motorcycle that day.

It was a smoldering Thursday afternoon in late May as I hurried through the warehouse in Simi Valley. Rushing down the long aisles of motorcycle parts, gas cans, and tires, I grabbed the tools and gear I thought would be necessary for the day's practice ride.

The paste-white industrial building had four large smoke-glass windows and an oversize roll-up door that housed all our race team's equipment. I selected a suspicious gas can off the shelf, knowing it was filled with high-octane performance race fuel, but I also knew that it was expired.

Just before filling the gas tank on my motorcycle, I paused. A vague, eerie feeling of doom swept over me and made me second-guess my afternoon plans. I was too excited though. In a hurry, I ignored the feeling in my gut and carried on.

I knew to never ride alone, and I usually never did. However, on this particular afternoon, there were no teammates or mechanics to go riding with and no one in the shop to tag along besides the office receptionist, Arleena.

How convenient, I thought.

I had a crush on Arleena, so this was a perfect opportunity to ask her to join me and role-play as my mechanic for the day.

With a smile, I approached her and gestured with a peace sign.

"Hey, Arleena, what's up?"

I greeted her with a high five, and she giggled as our hands clapped.

"I have a favor to ask, or more like an opportunity," I said with a laugh. "How would you like to be my mechanic today?"

I joked with her about being responsible for tracking my lap times with a stopwatch, checking my tire pressure, adjusting the engine idle, and more. Her rosy cheeks gave her away, and with a coy yes, we were off.

The bed of my tan single-cab pickup truck was crammed full

with a dirt bike, gear bag, gas can, and toolbox. We cruised with the windows down and the music up.

She turned to me and yelled out over the wind and song: "Since I'm your mechanic, you have to teach me how to ride your motorcycle!"

I nodded, winked, and pressed down on the accelerator.

It's funny what I remember of that day—everything that took place in the time between running down the stairs and into the garage to driving with Arleena is hazy. What is vivid, though, are the buckles that were on my black-and-white, carbon-fiber-and-leather riding boots. I'd put them on left foot first, then right, and then snapped closed from bottom to top as I had done numerous times before.

Many athletes have rituals or routines they go through in preparation for the risks they take. I was no different. I was religious with my methodic goggle cleaning and new-helmet rule—drop it on the ground and scratch it first before I wore it. New riding gear had to be stomped in the dirt and dirtied before wearing to hopefully prevent crashing and dirtying it the hard way. A humored Arleena looked on while I dressed in the bed of my truck and explained my superstitious routine.

The first few laps on the dusty track were belabored because of a nagging engine problem with the bike. I stopped a couple of times to adjust the carburetor before continuing on the racetrack, forgetting about the expired fuel I was using.

My confidence was high as I leaped through the air and carved through the soil. My body was one with the machine, sensitive to every vibration, every juxtaposition. I could hear and feel the rpm of the engine rev with power and explode with speed. I reacted to every bump, jump, rut, and rock without thought. I was in the zone.

I raced past Arleena with her stopwatch and yelled, "This is how it's done!"

I smiled inside my helmet. I was living my dream. I was racing a motorcycle and getting paid for it. The world as I knew it was in a tight grip between my hands, and I was twisting the throttle wide open toward the future.

At full speed, over sixty miles per hour, I shifted into fourth gear and readied for takeoff. At the most critical part of the launch ramp, I needed maximum power to launch me up and over the land obstacle. What happened instead was like a computer glitch. A momentary hesitation, a bog in the high-revving engine and the power it produced. The physics of the misfire flung me headfirst over the handlebars. There I was, in flight, three stories above the ground without my motorcycle beneath me.

"Ohhhhh shiiit!" I yelled as I fell.

As frightening as this scenario was to a bystander, it was not a foreign experience for me. I had fallen from great heights before and was accustomed to the consequences, most often broken bones. I distinctly remember my first. Again, a leap through the air on a motorcycle. However, it was not a crash—but rather a jump so high and far that the impact collapsed the plush shock absorbers on the motorcycle and crushed my feet into the ground. My right leg snapped from the force. I didn't even fall off the bike. I just rode off the track back to the truck and pointed at my crooked boot.

"I broke my leg! I broke my leg!"

Peculiar pain radiated through my body. It felt ice cold or scalding hot—I couldn't tell, but the throbbing was intense and familiar.

This was my memory while falling, a thought process rational enough to forethink trying to land in such a way as to avoid breaking the large bones in my legs. What didn't occur to me was breaking my neck instead.

SNAP! As loud as a gunshot, it echoed. The wet crunching sound of a snapping celery stalk is the sound that reverberates in my memory.

That sound was deafening. A numb, high-frequency hum.

I tumbled over and over, somersaulting down the dirt hillside. I could see my arms and legs flailing about wildly, uncontrollably. Sky, ground, sky, ground, sky, ground. It was a strange view of myself, as if I were watching someone else's body suffering this horrific fall.

There was no pain, no strain, no sensation at all. The chaos was over in mere seconds. As the dust began to settle, I rested quietly upon the earth among the stones and dry yellow grass. Conscious and very much aware of the horrific sound I'd heard, I thought ... *I just broke my neck! This is bad.*

Lying in the fetal position on my right side and looking through fogged, dust-filled goggles, I stared intently at my gloved left hand, which was resting directly in front of my face. I noticed a rock lying next to my hand.

Move! Move! Come on, hand, flicker, twitch, ANYTHING; just move!

The premonition from earlier in the day swirled around my mind as a sense of acceptance swept over me; I understood I was paralyzed. I would remain on the ground as still as that stone, indefinitely if no one came to rescue me.

Screams and shouts filled the air as Arleena and onlookers rushed to my aid.

"Aaron!" Arleena cried. "Aaron! Are you OK? Are you all right?"

She knelt in front of my face and looked into my wide-open eyes.

I whispered faintly to her with all the breath in my body, "Don't touch me, Arleena. Just call for a helicopter and paramedics. I just broke my neck."

She rushed off and quickly returned to my side moments later. I asked her to lie down and talk to me while we waited.

I was terrified. I could barely breathe; it felt like I was going to die right there in the dirt.

Arleena looked into my eyes and softly said, "You're going to be OK, Aaron. Everything is going to be fine."

Her voice kept me calm and was comforting enough for me to try to make light of the situation.

I whispered back, "That's *not* how to ride a dirt bike."

The corner of her mouth curled as she continued to rest alongside me.

Vwomp, vwomp, vwomp! I heard the thundering blades of the helicopter as it chopped through the air. It felt like its landing was sucking all the oxygen from my body. I soon realized it was not the helicopter, but me . . . I was suffocating under the weight of my paralyzed body.

"Where does it hurt?" the paramedics shouted. "What can you feel?"

I mustered enough breath to respond, "Don't take my helmet off. Just stabilize my neck; I know it's broken."

I was determined to keep my helmet on. For what? I don't know. Other than I felt safer with it on . . . and instinctively I knew it would hurt me much more if they were to tug and pull on it to remove it. They kept it on.

I begged the nurses in the emergency room not to remove my helmet as they used scissors to cut my pants and jersey off. My cracked helmet was still fastened to my head when a nurse waved a pointed safety pin in front of my face, telling me that she was going to prick parts of my body and wanted me to respond when I felt the sting of the needle. Without a view of her hand and the needle, I could not tell what she was doing.

After a few moments passed, I asked her, "Are you going to poke me or what?"

"I am!"

"Where?"

"Everywhere!"

That's not good, I thought.

Just then I felt a faint prick.

"Ohhh!" I winced.

"You can feel this?" the nurse asked.

"Yes, barely. It's my heel, the bottom of my right foot!"

A team of doctors swarmed in and began to remove my helmet. The bright-white halogen lights in the emergency room began to fade, along with the loud, chaotic sounds of voices and machinery. I began to flash back to my earliest memories and to the day I'd first laid eyes on a motorcycle. My last thought as I drifted away . . . *damn, they took my helmet off.*

THE REBELLIOUS RECOVERY

PART 1 # BEGINNING

AWARENESS

SURRENDER

INSPIRATION

COMMITMENT

SERVE & SHARE

"The quality of seeds we plant determines the garden we reap and sow."

The Gift

I heard the sound of sizzling sausage as the scent wafted through the house and awoke me early Christmas morning in 1982. My grandmother, Mimi, was downstairs at the kitchen stove, stirring a pan of homemade biscuits and gravy, my favorite breakfast. I have few memories from when I was three years old, but this one remains vividly intact. I can close my eyes and still remember jumping out of bed and rushing to the railing atop the staircase of my grandparents' living room. From the high second-story vantage point, my cheeks were pressed between the supports of the cold, black iron railing . . . my eyes still half-shut with sleep but clear enough to make out the anomaly in the room.

There it sat—a pint-size yellow-and-black motorcycle in front of the redbrick fireplace just left of the Christmas tree. This Southern California home was decorated with a massive tree . . . the type that fills a home with the smell of warm Douglas fir, adorned with colorful blinking lights and wrapped gifts bulging from under its sagging limbs. The hair on the back of my neck stood straight up from what I was seeing.

I had on my fire-engine-red onesie pajamas that allowed me to slide down the two flights of carpeted stairs as if they were snow covered. A hop, skip, and jump over the couch landed me onto the seat of that metal steed.

No amount of wrapping paper, bows, or ribbon could excite me more than that bare machine. It was custom built to my size; my little hands fit perfectly around the tiny black rubber handlebar grips as the motorcycle sat quietly, waiting for me to kick-start it to life.

I buzzed my lips: "Vroom, vroom, vrooooom."

I swayed forward and back, side to side on the bike. I could barely contain myself!

My grandfather, Papa, wheeled the cycle out into the large grassy yard behind the house. A long passenger train rumbled behind a row

4

of tall, thinly spired cypress trees as my dad fastened a set of pink training wheels to the rear of the two-wheeler.

I had played only on plastic toy tricycles, not yet having learned to balance a bicycle. At three years old I was about to leapfrog a pedal bike and go straight to a motorcycle, a man's machine.

I remember Papa telling me, "Son, if you can kick-start it, you can ride it."

Something magical happened the moment the full-face helmet and goggles were slid snugly over my head and face, Dad fastening the buckle under my chin. I peered out through the latex lens, my view narrow and focused only forward. I felt protected, imbued with strength and a powerful feeling of invincibility while inside that helmet.

I kicked and kicked until the machine revved to life. Without hesitation I twisted the throttle grip as far as it could go, rocketing me full speed right into the neighbor's wood fence. I was shaken and scared, but unhurt, and I quickly bounced up to mount again. In that moment where fear, courage, and control clashed together, I transformed into something more. I learned so young that I had the power to control my life with my will—the first seed planted and the beginning of my grand adventure.

Genesis

One Saturday night a couple of years later, while spending the weekend with my dad, he took me to the Monterey County Fairgrounds to watch flat-track motorcycle racing. The eight-mile dirt oval racetrack was encircled by a two-story, wood-sided grandstand with steep concrete stairs and beer-strewn walkways.

I was in awe at the sight, sound, and smell of thumping Harley-Davidson motorcycles as the racers slid their bikes sideways . . . three, sometimes four abreast around the oval. The fearless racers bumped and shoved each other at lightning speed as they jockeyed for position.

The winner crossed the finish line on his rear wheel, saluted the crowd, and taunted his rivals.

I remember seeing the leather-clad race winner carrying his trophy, walking among the fans in the stands. He strutted with a side smile and a hitch in his step that made his boot skid against the ground like a horseshoe on street pavement. I was completely enamored.

While I sipped a soda and ate popcorn, the announcer's voice echoed over the loudspeaker, calling the next race to the start line. Eight little riders and their peewee motorcycles, like mine, were wheeled out onto the track by their dads. My eyes widened.

"Little bikes, Dad!"

I couldn't believe what I was seeing! I desperately wanted to jump down out of the grandstands and join the race with the other kids.

That was the genesis, the moment my heart sparked and was set on motorcycle racing.

I begged my dad to take me back to the fairgrounds the next weekend. He loaded my little Yamaha into the bed of his pickup truck, and we went racing.

My nimble little body was perfect for motorcycle racing. Like a horse jockey, I was light, agile, and limber . . . and unafraid to twist the throttle wide open. I soon raced ahead of the other kids—because compared to the coffee cans in the field that Dad had set in a figure-eight pattern for me to practice, flat-track racing seemed easy. All I had to do was go fast and turn left.

Dad made the fairgrounds a weekly activity. Nothing compared to a race weekend. The first thing I did when we arrived at the track on race day was sneak into the trophy room and peek at the treasure I would race for. I'd keep the thought of the trophy during the race, which gave me an extra boost of confidence to twist the throttle a little harder and hang on a little tighter. I loved winning those shiny trophies that were, in most cases, taller and heavier than me.

I became mid-state champion in my division at six years old and was known at the racetrack as "Darin'" Aaron Baker. We raced almost every weekend for those first few years . . . until I had a scary crash that landed me in the hospital.

While lying on the ground after the accident, I cried about pain in my neck. The paramedic placed a stabilizing collar on me and rushed me to the hospital. The doctors, fearing I had broken my neck, immediately x-rayed my spine. An anomaly was revealed in the film. A small metal alligator clip was crimped to the skin of my neck, pinching me beneath the soft neck collar. During my fall, my little rainbow-color suspenders had become unclipped from my pants and reclipped onto my neck—which was the source of my tears.

This crash was enough of a scare for my mom to call an end to motorcycle racing. At eight years old, she retired my race helmet.

Ohhh, the contempt I held for the judgment. I rioted against her rule with tantrums and sulked for a long while after. There was no other activity that could compare to the thrill of my little motorcycle. A sense of dullness set in, and a feeling of loss and underlying resentment ensued.

Looking back at it now, that may have been the genesis of my rebellious nature.

Beyond the Helmet

My mother, Laquita Dian—I affectionately refer to her as "Toots" (a nickname I gave her as a little boy when I attempted to be cute to avoid a scolding)—and my dad, Dan, divorced when my younger sister, Arielle, and I were two and four years old (respectively).

I remember feeling torn between the two of them. I would kick, scream, and run off during parent-to-parent handoffs to avoid choosing sides. I had trouble sleeping, I wet the bed, and I was tormented by night terrors.

Their worlds were indubitably different. Dad's backyard, the rolling Steinbeck hills of Salinas, a fertile valley known for its rich agriculture . . . just inland from the Monterey Bay along the central coast of California, was my playground on the weekends. In San Benancio Canyon, I would ride until the ground was grooved and the gas ran dry. I loved going to Dad's on the weekends because, in addition to riding my motorcycle, I got to be his right-hand man at construction jobsites.

As a general contractor, he often took me to work with him and would teach me how to build things with my hands and chew tobacco. Just like him, I'd wear a little tool belt with a hammer and bag of nails. He'd show me how to hold a nail and swing the hammer, and how not to hit my fingers. I would be his helper and hand him tools—a screwdriver, pliers, snips, or clamps. Sometimes I even got to mix concrete.

I marveled at him as he climbed high up on the roof of a framed house. I thought he moved like Spider-Man. He and the other workers treated me like one of the guys and gave me a lot of freedom to do as I pleased.

During the school week Toots enriched Arielle and me with creative activities away from the motorcycle. With a waitress's wages, she nurtured us in the idyllic Monterey Bay, inspiring us to make adventures out of the mundane. The three of us often curled up together under a blanket next to a roaring fireplace while she read us the books *Where the Red Fern Grows*, *Adventures of Huckleberry Finn*, and *Oliver Twist*. On a tiny TV connected only to a VCR, we'd watch movies like *The Journey of Natty Gann*, *Lord of the Flies*, and *Pippi Longstocking*.

Inspired by the latter, Arielle and I turned our chores into theatrics by dressing up in every single piece of warm clothing we owned: wool hat, gloves, goggles, boots, and rain jackets to set off in search of treasure, like Pippi. We'd brave a steep, precarious trail, just beyond our front door, that descended two hundred feet down onto a small kelp-strewn beach cove to look for beach wood, pieces of smooth ocean glass, seashells, and jade stone—the same gifts Pippi's seafaring father would return home with. Five days a week during the elementary school year, our enrichment was simple—we sang songs, played music, read books, hiked, biked, and explored the coastline.

We moved from tiny house to tiny house, each one nestled in the sweetest little spots all around Monterey, Seaside, Pacific Grove, Big Sur, Carmel, and Asilomar Beach.

When the school bell rang, Toots set us free to roam with friends in the safety of our small artisan community. By bicycle, skateboard, surfboard, or Rollerblades, we'd explore every nook and cranny in and around town. The smell of moist ocean air and campfires still brings back fond childhood memories. Toots would frequently take us to the water's edge to picnic and camp overnight on the sugar-white sands of Carmel Beach. We frolicked upon the rocky shoreline and waded through shallow tide pools. I poked the squishy anemones and caught small, skittish crabs, splashed in the salty waves, built sandcastles, and buried Arielle shoulder deep in the sand.

One of my favorite places we lived in was a bright-red, turn-of-the-century Chinese pagoda that had originally been shipped to San Francisco for the world's fair in 1939. The authentic relic eventually came to rest nestled in the sand dunes by the sea in Asilomar Beach. The dune sanctuary became my playground, a soft sand cradle for me to test my flying skills.

I tugged on the frayed ends of a well-worn, king-size bedsheet, tensioning the knot tied around my left ankle just above my high-top sneaker. I looped the other corner around my right ankle and stood up, licked my finger, and raised it high in the air to check the wind. I tied loops in the other two corners of the sheet and slipped my skinny wrists through. With dangling folds of faded green fabric hanging off my back, my homemade wingsuit was ready for a test flight.

Like a monkey, I climbed up a thick cypress tree branch layered in chunky brown flake bark that arched like a rainbow high above the dune. I stood twenty feet atop the gently swaying tree branch with outstretched arms and legs. I counted three . . . two . . . one . . . then jumped!

The thick sea air caught my fabric cape like the thin skin of a flying squirrel and inflated the ballooned canopy behind me, just as I'd imagined it would. I soared down to the bottom of the steep dune, landing and tumbling with laughter in the warm sand. I sprang up, sand spilling from all orifices—my shoes filled and tiny beads fell from my hair and ears, down my back, and into my pants. Without hesitation, I scampered my way back to the top of the dune to jump again.

Across the Globe

In July 1986, Toots was inspired to embark on a journey across the globe. For reasons unbeknownst to us and with little warning, my sister and I held tight to her hand. Our uncle Keith was in tow as the four of us boarded a 747 jetliner bound for Tokyo. Toots's plan was to live on the Indonesian island of Bali, but she knew better than to tell us that.

My first-ever flight lasted over twelve hours and seemed to teleport us from one world to another so drastically that I could barely comprehend what was happening. Japan was hot, loud, crowded, and chaotic . . . and that was only a short stopover before we boarded another plane south to the southernmost tip of Malaysia.

The fairly advanced metropolis Singapore was located right on the equator. When we stepped off the plane, it was horrendously hot. The air was so thick and humid, it felt almost drinkable. From the window of the taxi on our way to the hotel, I was scared by the people bustling around the car. All walks of life seemed to converge in the streets without rules. Cars, trucks, motorcycles, and buses swerved around bicycles and rickshaws. Mules, goats, and even people pulled various-size carts full of goods. Children my age and younger in rags rushed to the windows to beg whenever the car stopped. I didn't understand why they were begging and why they seemed so poor.

Exhausted and hungry, our biological clocks were way off. Singapore was sixteen hours ahead of California, and we were wide awake. We wandered the city at midnight in search of something recognizable to eat. The sights and smells of Malaysian street food shocked Arielle and me. Toots and Uncle Keith thought it was funny to taunt us with skewers of mystery meat and cups of fruit pulp that smelled like flatulence. Hungry and hopeless that we would ever find a familiar meal, my eyes lit up at the sight of the McDonald's golden arches, which were awkwardly erected next to a street vendor. We begged Toots to take us there. And so, while on the opposite side of the world at two in the morning, Arielle and I sat in the streets of Singapore and gorged ourselves on American McNuggets.

The next day the four of us explored the outskirts by foot, rickshaw, and motorcycle, visiting ancient city ruins, a Buddhist monastery, and the Wild Things Zoo . . . where a giant orange orangutan, similar to King Louie from *The Jungle Book*, swung branch to branch looking for bananas.

Uncle Keith disappeared later that evening for what I assumed was adult time. We found him late the next morning passed out by the hotel pool under the savage Singapore sun. He was so sunburned that he was hallucinating. Three-quarters of his body was covered with water-filled blisters. Toots was angry and exiled him to the hotel room, where he soaked in the bathtub.

Still not acclimated to the time zone, Toots and I left Arielle with Uncle Keith in the room on our final day. We found ourselves meandering through the streets at 5:00 a.m. A colonial hotel lured us into its lobby, where we splurged on what Toots still remembers as "the best watermelon" she's ever tasted.

The next day we flew to Jakarta, one of the northernmost cities in Indonesia. Uncle Keith tiptoed through the airplane, squealing and wincing with every step because of his burns. Toots was still upset and had even wanted to leave him behind.

One night in Jakarta was long enough. We holed up in a decaying old motel room with one bed, no air-conditioning, and only a single dingy lamp shadowing the paint-peeled walls. Toots was adamant that we didn't drink the water or eat the food in fear of sickness.

Frightened, hungry, and anxious to keep moving, we boarded a suspicious-looking 1900s steam locomotive bound for southeastern

Java. The train was half-filled with passengers and half-filled with freight.

The faded green doorless passenger car creaked and rocked back and forth on rusty rails as we slowly passed by wood-shack villages and rice fields along the central Javanese countryside. A worn-out tan leather bench seat was our makeshift bed for the eighteen-hour island traverse. I sat with locals on the exposed step in the train car doorway with my feet dangling freely in midair, the ground speeding beneath me and the moist island wind whisking my face and hair.

Massive cobwebs encased a pipeline that closely paralleled the train tracks; giant yellow-and-black banana-size spiders lived among the orb webs and frightened me. To pass the time, a laughing Uncle Keith told me made-up stories about the spiders and frightened me even more. He also told me elaborate tales that built me up as a motorcycle race winner . . . only to end with a sadistic twist that left me crying and pouting.

Uncle Keith was handsome, talented, and hilariously funny, with a knack for physical comedy. I cautiously adored him. There was something in his eyes, a sparkle like my grandmother's that drew me in . . . but there was also a mischievousness in his smirk that I was wary of.

One story was about me winning a monster truck race and receiving a gold trophy . . . only to later be disqualified because I was caught playing with myself behind the grandstands.

I jumped up on the bench seat in the sleeping rail car and screamed, "No, I wasn't!"

Uncle Keith laughed and tickled me.

"I'm just teasing."

I calmed down for a minute, and then he blurted, "It was actually a motorcycle race!"

He got me again. Toots begged him to stop.

The time-warped train ride ended at the southeastern coast of Kalipura, Java. We then boarded a crowded ferry boat headed eastbound for Gilimanuk Harbor, Bali. The boat wasn't nearly as overstuffed as the dilapidated bus we would soon ride for six hours to our final destination, Denpasar.

During the ride, I learned how to eat and drink fruit from a plastic bag and ration our little resources. My sister, Arielle, with her blankie in hand, learned to NOT suck her thumb! The days of us being thumb-sucking, blanket-carrying toddlers were gone. We were now world travelers.

In Bali, our one-bedroom island hut was built from brown palm and stood on stilts above the golden sands on Kuta Beach just feet from the Balian Sea. Arielle and I played all day with islander kids, bodysurfed the waves, and swam with tourist children at the adjacent hotel pool. With sun-kissed skin and cornrow braids in our hair, we rode two-up on tuk tuk scooters through the dirt streets in town and looked more like locals than the pale tourists we had been when we arrived. We were loving the island life . . . then Toots tried to enroll us in school.

She escorted Arielle and me early one morning down a cobbled street to the schoolhouse, where the novelty of our month-long globe-trotting adventure quickly wore off. School was where home was, and home was not here. I missed my motorcycle and my friends and begged her not to enroll us. She instead brought us home.

Eclectic Influence

Not long after we returned from Bali, Toots married an eccentric man named Peterson. He had two boys of his own, four and six years older than me, a huge age gap at the time. My new family comprised dominant, well-educated world travelers who were very competitive guys. This new family dynamic challenged my former self-appointed role as the man of the house. I was now the little brother, the butt of jokes, physically overpowered, and sometimes teased and humiliated in front of friends and guests. This little-brother role made me despise and resent my stepbrothers and drove me further into my own interests.

I relished the fact that I was savvy on two wheels, though. Despite being the youngest boy, I could outride all of them on a bicycle. I could outjump, outmaneuver, and downright blow the doors off my stepdad and stepbrothers. It was my only real sense of confidence among them.

Peterson was an importer by trade and owned a gallery in Carmel: Conway of Asia. He and Toots traveled abroad together. They bought and sold antiquities—handwoven rugs and relics from Middle Eastern bazaars, Nepalese markets, Asian street fairs, and far-off shanties in nowhere towns and developing countries.

As a Partridge-esque family, we traveled throughout Europe and Central America. Exposure to more diverse cultures and eclectic food was an elaboration of the experiences Toots had inspired years earlier. There was no comparison, though, in the way we traveled now. I felt like little Kevin McCallister from the movie *Home Alone* as I was sometimes dragged along with my family through airports and hotels. Peterson helped us blend in. He spoke multiple languages and understood cultural etiquette, which allowed us to move smoothly off the beaten path to more unknown areas.

We spent nights deep in the Costa Rican rain forest in a hidden place high above a canopy, where the only access point was via a local farmer who'd pulled us in a wagon towed behind his rickety tractor. For hours we bounced down a sketchy mud road and across janky wood suspension bridges that crisscrossed the torrents of a rain forest river.

We ate handmade masa gorditas in mud huts with Guatemalan villagers near Maya ruins, and we frequented centuries-old châteaus throughout the Italian countryside. We scuba dived in the Great Barrier Reef and Great Blue Hole in Belize, and we caught and cooked lobster in a sand pit on an island no larger than a basketball court off the coast of Honduras.

We were always ready for adventure, our luggage never fully

emptied and always near the door. My passport was stamped full before the age of fourteen.

Our home felt like a museum, a catchall of imported goods from around the globe. Eight-foot elephant tusks framed the stairwell with a fully grown polar bear hide, head and all, draped over the banister. A twenty-foot python skin stuck to the living room wall, while a taxidermy cougar loomed in the foyer to greet guests. The massive Siberian tiger skin on the wall overlooked the dining room table with its gaping mouth, bared teeth, and piercing predatory stare. Aside from the handwoven rugs and ancient artifacts in every nook and cranny, the house was a Fish and Wildlife Service treasure trove. I would get lost in my imagination when sleeping on the couch near the fireplace, as a fully grown male lion—paws and all—draped over me as I slept.

Peterson and Toots hosted gatherings for all walks of life. Sometimes authentic American Indians graced our backyard with ceremonial sweat lodges. Drums, flutes, and sage smoke filled the air. I was the fire keeper, the one responsible for keeping the coals burning hot outside and delivering with a pitchfork the glowing red rocks into the lodge.

I knelt and ducked my head as I entered the lodge, tugging closed the cowhide that draped the entry. Aho! A deep bellow welcomed me into the darkness as the tribal elder rhythmically beat his drum. Ten or so bare bodies sat in a circle cross-legged, illuminated by flashes of fire that sparked off the glowing rock at the center. Dry sage leaf and sweetgrass were offered to the ancestors.

I crawled behind lodge leader Little Bear, Toots, and Peterson to find my place, the clay floor cool on my hands and knees. The heat was nearly unbearable and the air thick with smoke. I tried to stay seated and still but succumbed to lying low with my cheek pressed against the moist earth.

With my eyes closed I listened, entranced by the prayers and songs of the tribesmen. An hour passed, feeling like an eternity among the spirits. I emerged (feeling reborn) into the crisp night air. We danced and sang loudly around the lodge, my sweaty body lit by the fire against the moonless sky.

I knew it was going to be a party whenever our Afghan friends arrived. The house would fill with multiple generations of Afghanis laughing and singing around heaps of delicious kabuli pulao rice, potato bolani, and lamb kebab. I loved those nights around the table when we shared naan and ate with our bare hands.

Honestly, it took a couple of years in my early teens for me to really embrace the eccentricity of our life. I was often embarrassed, because everything from the clothes we wore to the music we listened to—even our food and general entertainment—was from another place and time. I had to reconcile the contrast of my life with Toots and my Carmel family with that of my dad, the motorcycle, and his suburban style.

Jumpers

One of my dearest friends, Mitch Sanchez, and I often holed up late at night in the tree house my dad built. We played guitar, wrote songs, and schemed up plans for new, more audacious adventures. The two of us were the most daring of our friends and loved skateboarding, gymnastics, and jumps from high places. We found semisafe ways to throw ourselves off my rooftop onto the trampoline and soar off cliffs into the river.

On a family road trip, we passed through Las Vegas and stopped only long enough for me to experience bungee jumping for the first time. As soon as I got home, I told Mitch about the jump, and we immediately got to work engineering our own homemade bungee cords.

We spent our allowance on spools of industrial-strength stretchy cord at the local hardware shop and began jumping out of a tree over the trampoline with the cord wrapped around our waists. Our boldness grew, and we soon began searching for a bridge to jump from.

The Mid-Valley Bridge was perfect. We took a height measurement, checked the depth of the water flowing under the bridge, scouted the best jump-off point, and tested the strength of the railing we planned to fasten our gear to. An escape route was mapped out just in case the police rolled by.

We cut our cords according to our measurements and sheathed it in brown ladies' pantyhose. We didn't know exactly what we were doing—but from the highest branch in the tree, we tested the cords' tensile strength and length based on our weight: 120 pounds each, soaking wet. We used professional rock-climbing harnesses with carabiner clips to secure the cords to our waists and ankles for the jump. Our backpacks bulged with cords and gear as we pedaled our bikes to the bridge. Our parents didn't ask where we were going because we were careful to stay out of sight.

As cars passed, Mitch and I fastened our cords to the railing of the bridge while looking over our shoulders to intercept any authority figures. Mitch wanted to jump first, so I had to be the lookout and the retriever. I had to winch him back up and over the rail once he had finished bouncing at the end of the cord.

Then it was my turn. The jump gave me a familiar euphoric rush. I felt like a bird in the sky, soaring through the air, absolutely free. Just like gliding down the sand dune or launching my motorcycle, I felt compelled to fly. Our legend grew, as word spread quickly among our friends. Our mothers didn't know what we had been up to until Toots read a headline in the local *Pine Cone* newspaper: "Teens Leap from Local Landmark." Apparently we were famous—but now we were caught and in trouble.

Toots grounded me for a month in an attempt to squelch my mischievousness. But she didn't specify what I could do with my time while confined to my room.

I happened to inhabit the downstairs living quarters, a large rectangular room with a full bathroom painted bright red, a half kitchen, and hardwood floors—plenty of space for the half-pipe skateboard ramp I sketched in my notebook.

Like an inmate hustling items in from the outside world, I had friends bring me wood and tools at odd hours. I built my indoor skate park while Toots and Peterson worked late at the gallery.

Within a couple of days, I was caught red-handed! But this time Toots couldn't help but be impressed by the ramps we'd built. So she somehow convinced Peterson to allow them to stay in the house.

Friends would come and go freely . . . so freely I'd sometimes come home to find them skating the ramp without anyone home.

Racing for Real

Because of my neck incident on the peewee motorcycle, it had been a handful of years since I had last raced or even ridden a motorcycle. I distinctly recall the day the motorcycle was reintroduced into my life.

It was November 1992 in San Francisco, California. My dad, my aunt Wendy's husband Uncle Joe, and I drove the two hours from Monterey up to the San Francisco Bay Area to attend a motocross event held at the iconic Cow Palace Arena.

The indoor event was loud, chaotic, and smoky—not a very pleasant atmosphere for the nonenthusiast. But for me the sight of neon motorcycles flying through the air and the sound and smell of the high-revving two-stroke engines immediately transported me to my early days of racing at the Monterey Fairgrounds.

I watched the riders with the same awe as I had years before.

I turned to my dad and said, "I want to race!"

I already knew how Toots felt about the motorcycle, but I asked anyway.

"I really want to race again," I begged her.

Toots was surprisingly supportive but had me sign a contract. It stated that I must maintain a 3.0 grade point average in school and promise to continue music and other sports. I gladly signed it, and so it began . . . an eight-year journey to the professional level—a road full of hard knocks, bumps, bruises, broken bones, and trophies . . . a lot of trophies!

On most weekends when my school friends were doing typical teenage stuff, I'd be out of town racing my motorcycle. I learned how to fix the bikes, trained in the gym, and focused on improving my race craft.

By sixteen, I had collected numerous amateur race wins, a CMA Grand National Championship title and two youth world championship titles—the most prestigious a Loretta Lynn AMA National Championship Number One plate.

The summer of 1995 was filled with some of my happiest memories with my dad. He and my grandpa Ed had just finished fabricating a custom race trailer for the long cross-country drive to Hurricane Mills, Tennessee, for the annual Amateur National Championships held the first week of August.

Loretta Lynn, the famous country-and-western singer, had held this iconic race on her property for more than twenty years. For the country's fastest motocrossers and their families, the weeklong event was a once-a-year destination, an all-in opportunity to showcase a rider's skill in front of corporate talent scouts and industry executives. This race was the equivalent of the World Cup for amateur racers and a must-win for future sponsorship.

The sprawling homestead held activities galore. There were rope swings and cliff jumps along a shallow river that ran through the forested pit area. Loretta's plantation-style home sat among cornfields as far as the eye could see and was open to the public for tours. A massive covered stage area held live music and awards ceremonies with an adjacent swimming pool for families to leisurely gather and barbecue. Off the track, kids were kids; we all played together, drove golf carts and mopeds through the mud, and made mischief wherever we went. Parents circled their motor homes like covered wagons and convened around firepits with beers in hand, discussing the weather, lap times, and race schedules. All was fun and games until race day.

Dad and I spoke very little the morning of my last race of the weekend; we were so tuned into each other and our prerace routine that we didn't need chatter. It was "go" time. The rain from the night before had turned the groomed dirt track into a swampy mess. Dad pushed my bike up to the starting line and positioned it far to the inside of the thirty-nine other riders.

With his arm around me, he said a prayer, patted me on the back, and said, "Good luck, son. You can do this, just like we've practiced . . . ride your own race."

The three-year-old inside me kick-started the bike to life.

This was my opportunity to become the words of the poster that hung above my bed: "I, Aaron Baker, will be a Motocross National Champion."

I'd thought those words every night and every morning for the past two years. I repeated them to myself as I revved my engine, ready for takeoff.

I blasted off the gate and shifted through the gears. I won the holeshot, the first bike to the first turn. As chaos ensued behind me, my adrenaline pumped. I twisted the throttle grip with all my might, muscling my machine through the mud ruts, bumps, and jumps. I sped toward the infamous Ten Commandments section . . . ten sequential jump obstacles known to separate the field. Lap after lap, I launched smoothly three at a time through the technical rhythm lane and held the lead.

As I rounded the final turn, I sang loudly inside my helmet, "I'M A NATIONAL CHAMPIONNNN! AHHHHHHH!"

I soared over the finish line jump with my fist in the air and landed to an ecstatic crowd of family, friends, sponsors, and scouts. Mimi and Papa were at the fence as I turned off the track and rode up onto the winners' stage. I dismounted and collapsed into a chair, my body boiling over from the heat and humidity. I tore off my helmet and boots. My feet were on fire!

I shook the bottle of sparkling cider champagne and popped the cork, showering my dad and the crowd on the podium. Then I emptied the remaining foam onto my socks. I hugged Dad and held the "Number One" plate high. It was our proudest moment together.

Distraction

In the months following that win, I felt a new level of confidence in life and definitely felt on top of my game, but I also began to feel a bit of burnout from racing. I wasn't focused and became distracted by the social influences of a punk rock era in the sport. The high-octane music festival scene in the late 1990s fueled a crossbred ethos that brought together athletes from all forms of action sports. My other interests, like skateboarding, music, and girls, became more enticing.

I needed to change some things in my day-to-day life to make it to the professional level in racing . . . which was still my dream.

Toots separated from Peterson and had moved down the coast to Malibu. She and Arielle lived there, and I frequently visited from Bakersfield, where I was staying. That is where I met Adam Bice, Arielle's Malibu High School boyfriend. Adam and I got along so well that he eventually spent more time with me than her. We had a brotherly bond and were inseparable. We'd parade with our other friends up and down the coast, seeking shenanigans. We'd skateboard, surf, and crash local parties. We'd explore the mountains, rivers, and valleys at the edge of the sea. Adam became my best friend and an inspiration away from the motorcycle.

A year later, in the winter of 1997, Toots decided to invest in an eighty-acre cattle ranch in a rural part of Oklahoma just a few miles down the road from her parents' estate in Purcell. Toots wanted to be close to her mother—my grandmother Mimi—while Mimi fought breast cancer.

This was a great opportunity for me to move away from Southern California and the social scene I was caught up in. I thought I could refocus on racing by living on a quiet, secluded cattle ranch to practice and train.

I used Toots's new land to map out a practice track. On the rust-red soil, I carved corners that weaved through old-growth maple trees, down natural water-washed ravines, up and over rolling hills littered with cow pies, and over jumps that soared bank to bank across fish-filled ponds.

My natural terrain motocross track was a boyhood dream come true and one I spent many hours on, burning fuel through a tiny carburetor hole one gallon at a time.

The reality of a racer's life was bittersweet—I had just turned professional in the fall of 1998, but without a primary sponsor I was making very little money racing weekend to weekend. I became a vagabond (a true privateer racer) and was still delusional from my amateur success. I lived hand-to-mouth on the road, slept on couches, and was constantly out of money. I bounced checks all over the country and mostly paid my way with a gas card. I usually ate microwavable burritos, Doritos, and Gatorade from truck stops and food trucks in California, Oklahoma, and Texas . . . wherever the race events were.

Between race weekends I worked odd jobs like construction, roofing, driving farm equipment, and hauling mobile homes. This lifestyle was far from the championship dream I'd held in my mind for such a long time. One time, I found myself daydreaming about the motorcycle while behind the wheel of a tractor as I loaded a thousand-pound round bale of hay onto a flatbed trailer.

"Heyyy, watch out!" Uncle Keith hollered, ducking out of the way as I haphazardly maneuvered the tractor and its heavy load.

"You watch out!" I rebuked, still agitated by my agreement to be a farmhand for the weekend instead of racing.

Opportunity Calls

On January 1, 1999, my phone rang.

JR's voice bellowed over the speaker, "Hey, Champ! Happy New Year! You interested in interviewing with a new race team in California?"

JR, my former race mechanic and riding coach, whom I hadn't seen in over a year, was a man I loved and respected . . . so I was thrilled to hear from him.

Without flinching, I exclaimed, "Absolutely! This was the opportunity I was hoping for!"

I didn't ask any questions. I didn't care who the team was or what manufacturer of motorcycle they sponsored. All I cared about was that this was my chance at racing on the big stage inside football and baseball stadiums around the country . . . supercross!

The meeting was set for an auspicious day . . . Saturday, January 23—my twentieth birthday.

I was scheduled to meet the race team—the riders, mechanics, and owner—in Phoenix, Arizona, at the then Bank One Ballpark stadium during the second round of the Supercross series.

Armed with $40 in my pocket and a gas card, I borrowed Toots's Honda Accord and left Oklahoma in my rearview mirror. Twelve hours later, in Albuquerque, New Mexico, my eyes became too heavy. I pulled into a truck stop off old Route 66 for a snack and a nap.

Under the fluorescent lights of the parking lot, I reclined my seat and fell asleep. Startled by a semitruck horn, I awoke late the next morning in a panic. I was supposed to meet everyone at noon, and my watch said 7:00 a.m. I was still six and a half hours away.

"Oh no!"

As my truck-driving Papa would say, "Son, you need to drop the hammer and grab some gears!"

Meaning . . . go fast. And I did! I covered the more than four hundred miles of wide-open interstate highway in barely over five hours. I skidded Toots's Honda sideways into the pit area at the stadium just as the clock struck noon.

I could tell immediately the team had an unconventional vibe—a bit counterculture compared to the highbrow, clean-cut factory race programs like Honda, Kawasaki, and Yamaha.

It was a short and very informal meeting; it was just long enough for me to know that I was a fit for their team. Again, I wasn't picky about the details, and I was already good friends with a few of the riders.

That afternoon I accompanied the riders and mechanics into the stadium for the prerace track walk to scout the course layout, jump obstacles, and dirt conditions. My stomach was full of butterflies as I spoke with my future teammates about how best to ride this or that section of the racetrack.

I wandered off alone for a moment to sit on a hay bale atop the finish line jump and closed my eyes to envision the track. I imagined myself jumping through the air with the checkered flag waving and me winning the race.

Just then, Tyler Evans walked up and queried, "Baker! What do you think? Should I double or triple this section?"

What he was asking was, should he jump over two or three track obstacles in one leap?

"If you can shift into third gear out of that corner, then you should have enough speed to triple it," I suggested. "It will be much faster!"

I gestured with my hand (impersonating a motorcycle) and buzzed my lips, implying an engine sound, "Brrrrrrraap! Braaap!" Tyler signaled back with a thumbs-up.

Out on the track with everyone, I was comfortable and in my element. We all spoke the same simple language of engine sounds and hand gestures that are unique to motocross. I felt accepted and respected by my peers and couldn't wait to race against them in the events to come. I signed the contract there in the pits and enjoyed watching the race later that night.

I returned to Oklahoma only long enough to pack my bags and board a plane to Los Angeles . . . my future was set.

TO MY YOUNGER SELF

Beyond the beginning of this story, the deeper message is to encourage my younger self to remember to breathe first. In any moment when I am feeling overwhelmed, anxious, scared, or frustrated, I can pause and center myself with a single breath. I can reset with this mind-seed—breathe in and exhale . . . and then again. In through my nose, deep into my belly, and out through my mouth, slowly. This is the *beginning* of self-improvement and adventure into the unknown. Breathe and then move. I call it "Being before Doing."

Scan the QR code and head to therebelliousrecovery.com/beginning for this part's complementary photo gallery.

BEGINNING

PART 2 **AWARENESS**

SURRENDER

INSPIRATION

COMMITMENT

SERVE & SHARE

"Self-awareness is the first step in healing and the greatest agent for change."

Raindrop

On that fateful May day in 1999 my planned future took a hard left turn—the proverbial fork in the road was unexpected and imposed on me without choice. And as my helmet was removed and the light began to fade, so did my motocross dream, my passion, and my identity.

The surgery lasted about six hours, I was told days later. A team of doctors led by neurosurgeon Dr. John Lee elected for an anterior incision (opening the front of my neck) to access the three damaged vertebrae in my spine.

My injury was considered a compression fracture, meaning, when I landed atop my head, the blunt force of the impact crushed my spinal column down (chin to chest)—fracturing the fourth and sixth cervical vertebrae and completely shattering the fifth.

According to the post-op notes, the team's first objective was to clear the bone debris from the injury site. My C5 vertebra had exploded into hundreds of tiny pieces and needed to be meticulously and very carefully removed to prevent further spinal cord damage.

This meant plucking and sucking shards of bone fragments that were lodged in the spinal cord and surrounding tissue. The dura, the protective sheath that surrounds the spinal cord, was torn by the trauma. This and the compression kinking, like bending a garden hose, of my cord were the main causes of my paralysis. The doctors' overwhelming prognosis was that I had a "one in a million" chance of recovery . . . of ever having the ability to move my limbs again. Or feed myself. Or walk. Or of ever living an independent life.

This general, statistical projection caused a schism between the doctors, Toots, and me—Toots later declaring: "You're not talking about my son!" She rebuked the claim, rebelled against the system, and shielded me—preventing a hopeless seed from being planted in my psyche.

> "It always seems impossible until it is done."
> —NELSON MANDELA

THE GATE KEEPERS

"You're safe now, Aaron, and doing so well. Don't give up!" "You never know how far you can go unless you try, right?" "Visualize your body and believe you can heal—the body is capable of miraculous things." "We honestly don't know how much function will return, but we're here to help you get as much as possible." "You're strong. You can do this!" "Become a student of your body, Aaron."

These were just a few of the many encouraging words from the hospital staff who cared for me early on and into rehabilitation. It was their compassion and composed nature that nurtured me at a time when my body was most fragile and my mind most vulnerable. I was scared and uncertain and fearful of my future, but because of those doctors, nurses, and therapists, the upward trajectory of my life was set in motion at my bedside.

Those caregivers are my unsung heroes—healthcare professionals who chose this line of work—noble empaths who not only saved my life but seeded me with optimism and hope and empowered me with knowledge.

I respect and admire these men and women, and I hope to show my gratitude by recognizing them and reminding these stewards of their power—as they are the gatekeepers of influence, the earth angels among us who protect and heal, teach and guide us up and forward, away from pain and suffering.

To stabilize my neck, my C5 needed to be reconstructed. The choice was to use cadaver bone from a bone bank. By combining donor bone with what was left of my bone, the doctors crafted and grafted a new C5 vertebra, which was securely plated between C4 and C6 with a titanium plate and five screws on the anterior (front) of my spine. This technically meant that those three independent vertebrae would now be a single, fused bone structure . . . stable enough for the rest of my life.

Dr. Lee was confident enough in his procedure that he did not require me to wear the common halo, a medieval device that screwed securely to the skull to prevent head movement. Instead, I awoke two days later with my head wedged between two foam blocks and my forehead securely strapped to the bed.

The bed was a unique medical contraption, having six-inch foam borders that surrounded my entire body like the chalk outline of a homicide. These barriers were meant to keep my limbs stable as the bed slowly rotated forty degrees, side to side.

My body needed to be rotated to keep my fluids circulating, especially in my lungs, because a common secondary complication to a high-level spinal cord injury like mine is pneumonia.

When fluid builds up in the lungs and cannot drain from the body, it can cause suffocation and respiratory failure.

Because of the paralysis, I was unable to breathe on my own. Hence, I was on life support. A ventilator breathing tube was affixed to my mouth. Fortunately, there was no need for a neck tracheotomy deep down my airway and into my lungs, as with some patients. The Darth Vader–sounding machine cycled inhalation and exhalation every five seconds to keep my oxygen saturation levels above 95 percent—the normal range being between 95 to 100 percent for a healthy adult.

A respiratory nurse visited my ICU room multiple times a day to check my levels and ventilator settings and to suction my lungs with a barbaric vacuum device like the suction wand at the dentist. This experience still haunts me. The vacuum hose was aggressively wedged down my throat and into my chest cavity; it was like they were trying to unclog a drain with a coat hanger. The suction itself felt like life was being sucked right out of me. That type of pain is difficult to compare and is an experience I would certainly rather not remember.

Six days after the accident, while in ICU, fully paralyzed and strapped to a rotating bed, intubated on a ventilator, and fed through a tube, I was about to go from bad to worse.

My lungs began to fill with excess fluid. The respiratory nurse I usually despised seeing was nervously welcomed that day. I was unable to speak because of the tubes in my throat, so trying to communicate my distress was futile.

I remember blinking desperately at my dad, who stood at the left of my bedside.

I tried to convey my fear with my eyes and tried to scream, "I CAN'T BREATHE!"

At that moment, just before the nurse was about to suction my clogged airway, a code blue emergency was called over the loudspeaker. The nurse frantically looked up, handed the suction wand to my dad, and hastily left the room.

NO! I thought.

We were alone. Dad and I stared at each other while he held the medical instrument that could save my life.

I pleaded with him with my blinks: "Help me, please. Help me, I'm suffocating."

I felt trapped under ice, out of breath and clawing at the few translucent inches between life and death. I saw the life support machine and the numbers that held my fate out of the corner of my left eye.

My heart rate dramatically hastened as adrenaline coursed through my veins. I felt a blinding rage inside as every cell screamed for air. Lying there paralyzed and dying felt like I was fighting against a straitjacket; the more I struggled, the less I could do.

The ominous beeping of the machine alarmed the room, but to no avail. No one but my father was there. I could see my oxygen level drop . . . 89, 88, 87 . . .

With one last look into my father's eyes, I let go. I felt my final heartbeat in my chest and heard the machine flatline.

The intense fight, my instinctive struggle to survive, gave way to a peaceful bliss. I released my grasp on life and exhaled into oblivion.

Instantaneously my awareness expanded outward in every direction and dimension. Like a supernova star exploding, I became consciously connected with everything, everywhere.

My reality as I knew it dissolved . . . literally. The physical walls of the hospital room, the building, my body, and the constructs of my mind began to merge. Analogous to a raindrop landing gently in the sea, becoming a part of the whole ocean, I was one . . . with all the universe.

"Beyond space, time, thought, and word is a vast,
unifying field of potential."

The infinite, omnipresent oneness to which most religions, philosophies, and scientific theories allude was my experience. All my interpreted life experience, learned behavior, history, and human understanding was irrelevant. I was without my physical body and a singular identity. I now felt like part of a singular consciousness in a vast expanse of pure potential, vibrating harmoniously together with a flowing sense of bliss. I truly felt as though I could manifest into anything, anywhere, at any time.

This experience lasted just over two minutes before the emergency room doctors resuscitated my body with a "Three, two, one, clear" shock to my heart.

I immediately experienced a heavy confined feeling as my awareness was slammed violently back into my paralyzed body. Although I was not yet conscious, I do recall a distinct sense of form, boundary, and restriction. Imagine trying to stuff a giant, ethereal genie back into a tiny bottle.

When the chaos calmed and I was again alive and stable, I opened my eyes for the first time—the second time in my life, so to speak. My vision was vivid, but different. I was still confined to the rotating bed and had a limited point of view. But what I could see seemed to be less solid and opaque. I saw life through a new lens of awareness—mindful awareness.

I glanced around the room, looking at walls that moments earlier had seemed to disappear. I felt like I had x-ray vision. I wasn't literally looking through the wall, but I understood the fundamental nature of the wall. I knew what it was made of—not wood, drywall, nails, and paint, but actually nothing at all. Literally, actually, nothing. Just vibrations of tiny particles that, at their core, were actually filled with empty space . . . nothing. The wall was just a temporary form of high-frequency energy in the vast expanse of pure potential . . . the space that I had just experienced.

I then looked up and to the right of my bedside directly into the sparkling green eyes of Toots. We locked eyes. I saw the universe in her gaze. Her love embraced me and assured me that everything was going to be alright. In that moment after death, and with the realization of the ephemeral nature of life, I finally understood that the two most important aspects of being alive are to share time and love.

The excerpt from the poem "To See a World" resonated with me:

"To see a world in a grain of sand and a heaven in a wildflower, hold infinity in the palm of your hand and eternity in an hour."
—WILLIAM BLAKE

In the end, all we ever have are time on this planet and love in our hearts. It is with our thoughts, words, and actions that we give these two precious gifts away. A reverence for life filled my mind and a sense of gratitude overcame me. At that moment, I recognized my future. No longer a professional motorcycle racer, skateboarder, surfer, snowboarder, mountain biker, or even a simple fisher, I realized that I was destined to do far greater things in my life than pursue my personal interests or ambitions; I was destined for things that affect people's lives, to have a future larger than myself, and to hold a vision of a long road to a greater good.

> **"Gratitude bestows reverence forever changing the way we think and see the world and each other."**
> —JOHN MILTON

And although this realization of my future was ambiguous, it was fundamental—I would now move through my life mindfully aware and hypersensitive to my highest values and truest virtues. With heightened awareness life became clearer and the simplest things important. I began to pay attention—a single breath became an opportunity to refocus and revere. I'd hear my heartbeat and remembered it going quiet—a reminder to always remain grateful for my body and my time here.

My priority was simple—to connect to life, to my loved ones, and to my body—the **B.A.S.I.C.S.**

> *"Everything in life goes back to the basics—it's the simplest way to find calm in the chaos and build your foundation."*

Breathe first.

Painted Toes

Day thirty-one began the same as the day before . . . I was abruptly awoken by the attending nurse on staff to check my vital signs and bladder catheter and turn me from a side-lying position to my back. By 6:30 a.m., the fourth-floor intensive care unit was buzzing with activity—intercom commands, alarm sounds, frantic voices, and the occasional clash or bang of a gurney bed or utility cart.

I despised waking up this way, especially because the few morning hours between 4:00 and 7:00 a.m. were my best sleep.

My routine started out at 7:00 a.m. with the hot, stale plastic smell of eggs served under a worn Tupperware lid . . . a smell that made my stomach turn.

The feeding tube down my throat had been removed, and I was now encouraged to begin eating solid food. But between the skin-crawling smell and the fact that my throat was still raw from plastic tubing, I could barely choke down applesauce and pudding let alone scrambled eggs or toast.

Weight continued to fall off my body. Before my accident I was a lean 145 pounds of muscle, but now I was a frightening one hundred pounds of skin, bones, and atrophied muscles; I looked gaunt, half-dead.

After the morning therapy session was over and I was back in bed, despondent and scared, staring out my window, Arielle entered the room with a small bag.

She walked to my bedside, leaned over, kissed my forehead, and then pulled up a chair next to the foot of the bed. Without saying a word, she began to unpack her bag.

I strained to see what she was pulling out, spotting only red, blue, yellow, and green. She carefully placed small bottles of nail polish on the bed. Her calm and quiet, yet playful, energy was apparent as she uncovered my bare feet.

"What the hell are you doing, sis?"

She glanced back at me with a devious smirk.

"Don't paint my shit!" I snapped.

Arielle blatantly disregarded me and grabbed my left foot.

"I'm going to paint your toes, bro."

She giggled and dipped the brush into the sky-blue nail polish. I watched with rage as she made her first brushstroke onto my left big toe.

In my mind I was kicking her away and just then she said, "If you can kick me, I'll stop."

Oh, the agony! That moment was both endearing and agonizing. I loved that my sister playfully intended to cheer me up, but my inability to defend myself was a real heavy dose of reality . . . I really was paralyzed.

As the last stroke of bloodred polish covered my right big toe, Arielle stood up and stepped back to marvel at her masterpiece.

"There, that's better," she said proudly.

I lay there with disdain, skinny and pale, with ten toes as bright as a rainbow. All the colors of light combined on two paralyzed feet. I stared at my candied toes, perplexed and pissed off, yet slightly pleased with their color.

This is how my recovery from paralysis began. I was going to channel my anger into these focal points.

As an athlete, I used visualization as a way to imagine the perfect technique on the track. Before the race began, I'd close my eyes and see the track . . . every corner and every jump. I felt the handlebars in my grip, swaying side to side as I flowed around the course with perfection.

The intellectualization of my intentions became my first exercise in reconnecting to my body after injury. And although I had no prior anatomy education, I visualized the inner workings of my skeletal, muscular, and electrified neurological systems.

I imagined the color blue from my left big toe traveling up my leg into my torso, filling my chest, and swirling up my spine through the injury site in my neck and into my brain. I did this with the color red for my right leg, yellow for my left arm, and green for my right. All these colors swirled in my mind and created a bright, white energy that I forced throughout my body like a rainbow prism.

VISUALIZATION

Is seeing, feeling, smelling, sensing, and experiencing something in your mind, exactly as you would in real life. Visualizing triggers the same processes in your brain as a real-life experience would—transmitting the same energetic frequency and vibration through and around you. Therefore you can influence whatever you want to create in life, through visualizing it first.

Days after Arielle painted my toes—wiggle wiggle—my left big blue toe began to twitch. Again I whispered to myself. The color blue beamed through my body and down my left leg . . . again! My mind laser focused on the toe . . . again! Like a spark plug, I exploded a neurochemical impulse from my brain into my body . . . again!

> **"You have power over your mind—not outside events. Realize this, and you will find strength."**
> —Marcus Aurelius

I lay there staring at my blue toe, twitching it on command. Just then my mother entered the room.

"Look! Look! Watch what I can do!"

I was beaming with pride, excited to show Toots this new flicker of hope.

She threw her hands in the air and yelled, "Yes! We can do this, buddy."

It was that moment that we both knew recovery was possible. To what extent, we had no idea.

I showed everyone who entered the room my new ability, also proudly showing off my colorful toes. My toes became the focal point for conversations of optimism.

However, my neurosurgeon did not seem quite as excited as we were. To the contrary, he wanted to prescribe medication to subdue the spasms in my muscles to "make me more comfortable." I argued that although my muscles were spasming involuntarily, I could close my eyes and feel the contractions—essentially connecting my mind to my body. This was yet another cause for the chasm to grow between the doctors and me.

I refused to take any medication that would dull my senses or impair my ability to heal. Ever since my near-death experience, I was living a new level of sensitive self-awareness along with a powerful understanding of energy and its flow to and through me. I understood that my entire body was energy, and that every cell was intelligent. My job was not to lie passively in bed, numb on medication, but to instead focus my mind and orchestrate the flow of kinetic energy throughout my body. I needed to act; I knew nothing would work unless I did.

After all, it's a cliché for a reason—*Action Changes Things!*

I began to imagine healing with every breath. My mantra became, "Thank you, body. I love you."

My long road of recovery began with that single flicker. And like Dad used to say, "Baby steps, son. One at a time, we'll get there."

It was an endearing sentiment, and one I still use today. But for some reason I imagined these flickers of connection as Lego bricks from my favorite childhood pastime. My body was being rebuilt one colorful brick at a time, stacking flickers on top of each other to create tiny movements.

The quote by Martin Luther King Jr. was a perfect depiction of my perspective. I actually entertained an addendum to his thought:

> "If you can't fly then run, if you can't run then walk,
> if you can't walk then crawl—*AND if you can't crawl,
> then think about crawling*—but whatever you do,
> you have to keep moving forward." (Text in italics
> belongs to the author.)

Touch Assist

Imagine ET's glowing finger—you know, the famous extraterrestrial from the 1980s classic? Yes, that finger. Now imagine that finger slowly touching the left temple of my head, as I lay flat, faceup in bed. With my eyes closed, the finger touches my left temple, softly. A voice asks, "Can you feel my finger?"

I respond, "Yes."

The finger then moves to my right temple. "Can you feel my finger?" "Yes."

The finger then crosses down and over to the left side of my neck, again asking, "Can you feel my finger?"

And I again respond, "Yes."

This single touch-and-response technique continued over my entire body—crisscrossing from left to right down my neck, shoulders, arms, elbows, wrists, fingertips, hips, legs, knees, ankles, and toes, then back up through my torso and onto my temples again. And when the finger touched an area of my body that I could not feel, the finger would push harder, tickle, pinch, or move gently across my skin until I'd acknowledge, "Yes, I can feel your finger."

The finger belonged to my mother, or father, or whoever felt inclined to engage in an active meditation of this type. They'd stand at the bedside, often barefoot (for grounding), and perform the exercise that could last an hour or more.

This esoteric technique (originally developed in 1950s scientology) was meant to transfer energy from a giver to a receiver through a very focused point—with the purpose of establishing a communication or reconnection to the body.

Touch Assist was introduced to my family and me by a random man my uncle brought in to the hospital for a visit. And although scientology was foreign to us, the technique resonated. I found great value in daily practice. The simple activity sharpened my focus and amplified the visualization I was already doing. In fact, by feeling ET's finger pressing down onto me, my sensitivity heightened, and my ability to actually *feel* improved—not to mention the calming, meditative effect it had on my mind.

This unconventional exercise was another way for me to think differently about recovery—to envision my nervous system and to imagine electricity as bolts of lightning—arcing and sprawling throughout my body. A true reconnection.

> "If you want to know the secrets of the universe,
> think in terms of energy, frequency, and vibration."
> —NIKOLA TESLA

The Power of Sound

From the flicker of my left big toe to the twitch of my left leg, each day I expected to experience new movement. This, however, would not be the case. Recovery from a spinal cord injury is a long, arduous road of physical pain, suffering, setbacks, and patience—a roller coaster of mental anguish. And although I was flickering my toe and felt on the fast track of recovery, I couldn't even scratch an itch on my nose. I relied on others for every single one of my needs . . . bathroom, bathing, dressing, and feeding. This drove me crazy! The rage in my chest burned like a coal. I swung from one end of the emotional spectrum to the other, feeling moments of pure bliss, gratitude, and reverence for life . . . only to suddenly be set ablaze with anger and sadness.

In an attempt to create a serene environment to keep me focused on healing, Toots decorated my hospital room with a live green plant, a trickling water fountain, and a music player that played the soothing sounds of rain forests, American Indian flutes, Tibetan chants, and the ocean. She transformed the stale, cold room we shared into an oasis, a warm vortex of positive energy for a calm mind.

Also, a sound alchemy of Hemi-Sync tones and binaural beats was played through headphones as a way for me to relax my hyperactive brain—the idea being to evanesce from the waking state of gamma and beta wave frequencies, down to the lower and slower vibrations of alpha, theta, and delta—the deep-sleep realm—rapid eye movement (REM) for healing and restoration of mind and body.

CYMATICS

The study of wave phenomena, especially sound, and their visual representations. A therapy in which sound waves are directed at the body with the aim of promoting health.

I needed an outlet for my pent-up energy, though. So I began a new tactic during therapy sessions. I had her replace the soothing sounds with the darkest, loudest, and heaviest metal music she could find. My room pounded with drumbeats and guitar riffs. Primal screams echoed through the halls, likely scaring other patients in the ward. This sound was the sound of my soul screaming out.

> **"Music is what feelings sound like."**
> —GEORGIA CATES

I began to channel this sound through my body. Like the colors from my toes and energy from the finger, the music amplified my efforts by one thousand percent. Every exercise repetition was a cataclysmic explosion of willpower blasted from my brain into my body. The effort I made to achieve a single biceps curl was equivalent to someone attempting to lift a car. This masochistic mindset made good use of otherwise self-destructive negative energy. I'm sure my physical therapists thought I might be slightly mad—but that was OK, because at the end of the day I lay in bed content with my effort.

A poignant moment early in my recovery was when I was able, barely, to lift both my arms up from the side of the bed and wrap them around Toots in a delicate hug. With tears in both our eyes, she told me that she'd never leave my side and that hug was the best gift I could ever give.

That was progress.

Be Your Own Poster

The ballpoint pen was haphazardly Scotch-taped to my right hand, while both of my arms were strapped tightly to what Michelle, my occupational therapist, called "skateboards"—two shallow plastic forearm troughs with wheels underneath that allowed me to scoot my frail limbs across the table surface. I scoffed at the term "skateboard" while wiggling my noodle-like arms back and forth. "I loved to skateboard! On a *real board.*" I sulked.

She positioned a piece of blank white paper under the tip of my pen. "OK, Aaron. Let's see how well you can write."

"Errr." I begrudgingly began to score the paper, and then I stopped and remembered something Toots had told me years before.

> **"Be your own poster. Write down your goals, or hang a picture of yourself doing what you love."**
> —LAQUITA DIAN ("TOOTS")

As a young teenager she had printed a poster-size photograph of me airborne on my snowboard and hung it on my bedroom wall to replace an image of an obscure idol.

I recalled that lesson and the poster I'd made for my motorcycling dream and refocused on the paper in front of me. "I Will Walk!" I declared while marking the blank page with faint black strokes. My pen quivered as wheels of the skateboard crinkled the edge of the paper. "Let's hang this in my room where I can see it, Toots."

"Perfect!" she replied. "I'll need some of that Scotch tape, Michelle." Toots feigned a smile as they peeled the pen from my hand.

By penning that poster I was essentially taking my first literal action step toward manifesting what was in my mind. The simple act was the expression of my awareness, the thoughts I held, and my intention for the future. It was my sigil—a signpost to remind me of my direction.

> **"Writing down your goals is the first step in turning the invisible into the visible."**
> —TONY ROBBINS

TO MY YOUNGER SELF

My first couple of breaths are automatic, but my next few are focused. I intentionally turn my attention onto my breath and visualize a flow of energy throughout my body, and by proxy a connection is made. This is the initiation of mindful self-*awareness*—an expansive space of pure potential, the greatest agent in healing and change.

Scan the QR code and head to therebelliousrecovery.com/awareness for this part's complementary photo gallery.

BEGINNING

AWARENESS

PART 3   SURRENDER

INSPIRATION

COMMITMENT

SERVE & SHARE

"The ultimate act of power is surrender."
—KRISHNA DAS

The Threshold

After nearly six months of inpatient physical therapy, my insurance coverage was depleted, and the time had come for me to be discharged out of acute care at the hospital. There was a problem, though. Toots's house was in Oklahoma and Dad lived in Arizona. I had been living as a guest of people, and I didn't have a place to go. It didn't matter, though; I had to leave.

My family decided that the best and quickest option was to stay at a motel nearby. The hospital room that Toots and I had called home was packed up, refrigerator and all. The entire staff from the fourth-floor rehab unit gathered for a ceremonial send-off, ushering Toots and me to the sliding front doors.

My goal from the beginning had been to walk out of rehab to cut my hair. I wanted to recover 100 percent and walk into a barber, but I was far from that number . . . maybe more like 30 percent recovered. I was strong enough, though, to stand for short periods of time with help . . . my low blood pressure was a constant issue that caused total body weakness, nausea, and faintness to the point of blackout.

And so there I stood . . . with shaggy long hair in plaid pajama bottoms, with my neck securely braced, both legs braced from my ankles to my hips, my torso wrapped tightly in an abdominal binder with a bulky forearm walker—and Toots—ready to help me balance. Together, we stepped over the threshold from the safety of the hospital into a frightening, unknown world.

After a few tiny, arduous steps, I collapsed back into the wheelchair.

Motel Madness

It had been a very long time since Mom and Dad shared any common ground. I cannot remember the last time there wasn't tension between them. At this point, though, all their personal history and ongoing grievances needed to be set aside for the next step . . . leaving the hospital.

The transition from the well-equipped hospital to a bleak motel room was traumatic in every way, to say the least. It was here that I would begin my slow, insidious descent into darkness.

The first night on that hard mattress was a nightmare. My body was propped in a side-lying position with pillows all around to soften the pressure points on my tailbone, elbows, and shoulder blades because I had developed pressure sores in the hospital. I still wore the tight Philadelphia neck collar to keep my spine stable to prevent reinjuring myself. The neck brace gave me an odd sense of security; it was the only safety I felt at that point.

I became excruciatingly nauseated, maybe from stress or blood pressure drops; I'm not sure . . . but it was relentless. A tiny ice bucket sat next to the bedside and reeked of sour bile. My body temperature fluctuated from hot to cold; I was sweating and dizzy one minute, then shivering and chattering my teeth the next. My blood pressure kept rising and falling, which made the nausea, head spinning, stomach turning, body tingling, and deadweight feeling even worse. The vicious cycle continued through the night, compounded by the fact that my face itched from the starchy communal pillows and I could not scratch it myself.

I stared into darkness as reality began to creep in. I was no longer cocooned by the insulation of the hospital. The environment now felt very unsafe. The undeniable fact that I was completely unable to do anything for myself scared the hell out of me. This realization had eluded me in the first months after my accident with so many people at my side. But now, with Toots asleep and no one else around, the gravity of my situation sank in.

I was screwed. If all hell broke loose, I was totally effed.

I was an inanimate object, like the chair in the corner of the room.

I wasn't going anywhere unless carried or pushed. My chest and throat began to tighten as the panic overcame me. Beads of sweat slipped down my forehead and into my eyes, turning tears into burning bulbs that rolled across my cheeks and into my ears. I cried myself to sleep.

The following few days were a blur. As days slipped into nights and nights into days, I could not distinguish the time. Life outside my motel door seemed to move way too fast for my comprehension. All I could retain, faintly, was that my mother was by my side and my father was somewhere trying to find us a place to live.

A Familiar Dwelling

The pastel-white-with-green-and-brown-trim, adobe-style apartments nestled against the rolling yellow-grass hills in Westlake, California, was a familiar area for me. Two years before, I had lived in these apartments with my dad while attending Westlake High School down the road. The Knolls were the closest thing to home we could find. So close, in fact, that we rented the apartment next door to our former abode. It was an exact floor plan replica, just flipped.

The ground-level, two-bedroom space was fully accessible without modification and superbly accommodating of my new bulky electric wheelchair. However, the painful memories of my preinjury life were everywhere.

The dark-brown outdoor gazebo where I'd stored, washed, and worked on my motorcycles before a race weekend with my dad. The stairs and curbs were still abused and worn from when I'd used them to turn tricks on my skateboard. The glass-walled racquetball court, peanut-shaped swimming pool, and Jacuzzi I'd frequented with friends.

Although this place wasn't my childhood home filled with memorabilia, the haunting memories of my past self began to erode my optimism.

A month after being discharged, Toots, Arielle, and I were all together again under one roof, with Dad periodically visiting from Arizona to help out. All three of them, plus my childhood friend Adam Zerbe, from Carmel, took turns as my personal care attendant—catheterizing my bladder, relieving my bowels, feeding, bathing, dressing, and transferring me to and from a wheelchair . . . all day, every day. I was a helpless infant at twenty years old, and this complete dependency drove me deeper into the darkness.

Adam's father, Carl, graciously let us use his adapted van, nicknamed the Yellow Submarine. Carl had polio and thus owned a van with a wheelchair lift. When Adam and I were young, we took many road trips with his family in that big yellow beast—like to Yosemite and Pinnacles national parks. I remembered Carl in his electric wheelchair being hoisted up through the back doors by the squeaky mechanical lift. As kind and necessary as Adam and Carl's gesture was, it devastated me every time I wheeled onto the lift platform; I was so embarrassed and angry that I now needed the squeaky lift.

Adam drove me to and from outpatient physical therapy six days a week in the van for three months, selflessly caring for my every need. I felt terrible that he was giving up his freedom for my incarceration. There were long hours before and after therapy sessions that we just sat together bored indoors, with me in my big navy-blue recliner chair and him on the couch.

The recliner was one of three places you could find me—my bed, a wheelchair, or the Cadillac of recliners equipped with a cup holder, vibration seat, speakerphone, and remote control to raise and lower me. Once I was transferred into that chair, I remained there until moved back to a wheelchair or carried to bed.

Video games and an electronic music box with big buttons and knobs filled most of my time when I sat in the recliner. I masked my depression with occupational therapy . . . well, at least that was my excuse to myself and my family.

Inside I was crumbling away; day after day, my light dimmed more and more. Friends visited, scooped me out of my recliner, and took me for a drive, dinner, movie, or, even worse, a party. Family members tried to console me with platitudes masked by smiles. I saw right through the fear and fragility of my loved ones, the insecurity of my friends, and the superficial drama of the world. I was losing interest in everything; my previous colorful outlook on life's adventures became gray, while my gaze became long and lifeless.

Ten months into my new life as a quadriplegic I went to physical therapy two hours a day, five days a week. This was a dramatic decrease in treatment time compared to the regimented seven-hour physical and occupational therapy days I'd experienced as an inpatient.

The bottom line was my insurance carrier had deemed me rehabilitated. Wiggling my toes had lost its luster, and I craved more and more just to get out of bed. I spent most of the day struggling against gravity, spilling my meals, and soiling myself.

One such incident happened during a guys' night out. My friends, in an attempt to cheer me up, took me out to a dance club. I sat amid the dancing crowd in my large archaic wheelchair, the techno music pulsing loudly over my voice.

"I think I need to go to the bathroom," I yelled over the music.

Mikey, a dear friend from Carmel, nodded and kept his groove. He then summoned a pretty young lady to accompany me as I slumped dejected on the dance floor. She twirled and dipped around my chair and ran her fingers through my hair. She then sat heavily on my lap.

"No, no, no, ohhh nooo!" I cried.

She jumped up, but it was too late . . . my bowels released all over me and the chair.

These incidents enraged me, and I lashed out with intensity and then sulked in silence.

I couldn't make heads or tails of my feelings. The contrast of emotions was so vast and dramatic that I could swing from elation to fury in a moment. One minute I'd be thrilled to be holding a spoon, and the next I'd be livid, having spilled applesauce all down my face. In therapy I'd stand up with pride and hold myself without assistance, and at the same time cry as I stood in a puddle of my own urine. My line of sanity was so fine I continuously slipped side to side. It was exhausting . . . not only for me, but for everyone around me as well.

My dad came into my bedroom one day and lay down next to me as I was propped up in bed, staring at the wall. My mind was so empty and dark that I had not said a word to anyone in over a week.

He turned to me with swollen eyes and said, "We'll get through this, son. Just like when we were racing, we had our good days and our bad days. We'll get through this too. I'll be your hands, I'll be your right hand, I'll be your left, I'll get what you need."

Wiping tears from his eyes, his voice trembled. I remained cold, distant, and disconnected from the moment.

Toots, too, although she constantly encouraged me, was frightened by my disposition and began removing sharp objects from my room and around the house. It really didn't matter, though; I couldn't grasp anything forcefully with my dysfunctional hands.

The end seemed inevitable. All sounds were monotoned and muffled. Food was an inconvenience, and I refused water. I wanted out of this body, out of the dark and into the light. The place I'd been before. A blissful death was what I imagined and how to do it was my only thought.

Gravity Is Heavy

Three hundred and sixty-five days were long enough—the one-year anniversary of my accident crushed the remaining light in me. The burden I felt was so heavy, it dawned on me that gravity was literally going to be my way out.

For the past seven months, aquatic therapy had been a major part of my recovery. Generally, two therapists strapped foam flotation devices around my arms, legs, and torso and then gently lowered me into the water and floated me around in therapeutic ways. I knew that without the buoyant foam, I'd sink like a rock. This was a frightening reality and a fear I had to overcome during my sessions.

The bean-shaped pool with warm, chlorinated water was only a stone's throw away from our condo at the Knolls apartment complex. The place where only a short time before I had swum, sunbathed, and soaked with friends on hot summer nights was now a morbid exit plan in my mind.

Sometimes I would leave the house without telling anyone and drive around the neighborhood in my lime-green electric wheelchair. These were tearful tours, during which I steered my chair by joystick past the pool, racquetball courts, and sets of stairs I'd once effortlessly flown down on my skateboard. I'd grit my teeth, scream inside, and then cry, swerving like a drunk on the sidewalk with tears rolling down my cheeks.

I left the house again unannounced and rounded the sidewalk corner as a woman exited the gated pool area. I could not open the self-locking, heavy metal gate on my own. I called out to the woman, asking her to hold the door for me as I passed through.

I was alone. There were no kids splashing, families barbecuing, or sunbathers. As I rounded the pool, my wheels bumped over the cracks in the concrete. Heat radiated from the light-gray deck. I maneuvered my wheelchair to the lipped edge at the deep end, my front wheels less than an inch from the water.

Eight feet of water, an abyss for my two-hundred-pound electric wheelchair.

Tears stained my face as I stared into the glassy water, my reflection staring back. My mind was black.

Ambiguous, muffled sounds of life played out around me as I sat at the edge of the pool. The day's end drew near; the warm sun was setting behind me as cars began entering the parking lot, steered by weary professionals returning to their apartments from a long day's work. In that moment I saw nothing . . . no future for myself, no purpose, and no reason to continue.

In my darkness there was, however, a single fleeting thought—the memory of my mother's eyes staring into mine the moment I'd woken up from my near-death experience. I remembered how her eyes, like my grandmother's, flickered like starlight, bright like the sun, beaming with all the secrets of the infinite.

I sat there for what felt like an eternity, locked in an internal battle over whether to go or to stay. The slightest muscle spasm, untimely sneeze, or rash decision to tap the joystick would have sealed my fate. But the longer I sat, the stronger that memory grew.

Her eyes flashed in my mind again. I suddenly pulled the joystick in reverse, backed away from the edge, turned my wheelchair around, and sobbed. I surrendered. I hit bottom. Aside from suicide, I couldn't go any lower. This was the bedrock upon which I would rebuild my life—**the bottom; a dark, bleak base from which to push up from.**

TO MY YOUNGER SELF

With my eyes closed and my attention turned inward, I relax. I let go and *surrender* to the present moment, whenever and wherever I am. I release my mental grip on the expectation I have for the future or a repeating memory of the past, and allow my thoughts to pass like clouds in the sky. If I am in pain, then I lean into it and listen, quietly . . . my breath is the only thing that can guide me through.

I repeat these three steps as often as I need throughout my day—Breathe, Awareness, and Surrender. By doing so, I tune in and align my mind, body, and spirit. I become present and poised before doing. This is a way of being calm, connected, and ready to act. Action changes things!

Scan the QR code and head to therebelliousrecovery.com/surrender for this part's complementary photo gallery.

BEGINNING

AWARENESS

SURRENDER

PART 4 **INSPIRATION**

COMMITMENT

SERVE & SHARE

"Breathe first, then lean in, let go, and look up—toward the future and the space of infinite possibility."

Love Is Tough

I was sitting in the corner of the living room, in my recliner chair, when Toots walked through the front door.

"I don't need you!" I screamed. "I don't need you like this!"

She had just found her way home from her own abyss—a four-day alcohol-induced bender at the border of Mexico; she never made it to Oklahoma. This was her edge of the pool, her rock bottom—literally. She'd found herself facedown in a gutter in Calexico after being released from an overnight stay in jail. After a sobering bus ride back to reality, she entered the house where I sat and cried.

"You may not need me, Aaron," she said. "But I need you, and I need to stay."

I was seething with anger. I despised seeing her drunk. How could she do this to us? I yelled at her. I wanted her as far away from me as possible. Yet she stood her ground. Toots swayed me to let her stay.

After all, my dad may have once said that he would be my hands, but it was Toots who literally was. Up to this point she had never left my bedside. She was there from the moment I awoke in the hospital to now, living with and caring for me 24/7. *What was the alternative?* I asked myself. I knew we needed each other in order to keep going.

We reconciled enough to have pulled back from the edge that day, but we were still painfully fragile and in desperate need of help.

A few days later, June 2, 2000—a little over twelve months after the accident—Toots made a unilateral decision to change our depressed circumstance. With forceful action she burst into my room and muscled me up and out of bed and carried me to the car. I was still angry at the fact that I couldn't fight as she belted me into the seat.

"What are you doing?" I screamed. "Where are we going? I haaaaaate this!"

A torturous aspect of my injury was that no matter how I felt, what I wanted, or didn't want, I was dependent for everything. I could speak my wishes but couldn't act. The fact was that life would carry on around me, whether I liked it or not.

As Toots drove, she sternly said, "We are going to the Center of Achievement."

She knew that our insurance coverage was ending and had already researched the next feasible step for my ongoing physical therapy, having uncovered two potential opportunities. One, an aquatic program on the other side of the country, for which we didn't have the money. Two, a more local place referred to us by Andy Bray, my friend and former roommate in the hospital (who also had a spinal cord injury).

I didn't know what she was talking about and didn't reply; I just sat angrily for the thirty-minute car ride. I sulked further with my head down as she pushed my wheelchair past droves of beautiful young students down a long pea green linoleum-floored hallway at California State University, Northridge, where the therapy center was.

At the end of the corridor on the left was an unassuming closed door with a small square plaque that read in embossed red writing: THE CENTER OF ACHIEVEMENT.

Toots wheeled me through that door and into the brightly lit kinesiology lab, where both our lives changed instantly. Like being bathed in beams of angelic light radiating from above, we stopped in awe at the entry. In that moment, the "door effect" became central to our mission of making sense out of our tragic reality.

The floor was covered wall to wall with bright-red carpet; mirrors lined the walls and reflected silhouettes and smiles of people exercising on unique and specialized equipment—the likes of which I had never seen before. The room was abuzz with activity; my eyes widened, and the corners of my mouth turned up. I felt my smile as an empowering spark of possibility entered my mind.

A tall, imposing figure dressed head to toe in black-and-white Adidas apparel with a black bandanna around his head that tamed a long, curly ponytail appeared from around the corner.

With his hand extended and a thick South African accent, he exclaimed, "Hello, I'm Taylor Isaacs. Welcome to the Center of Achievement!"

"Hi, I'm Aaron Baker. I hope you're the one that will help me fix my tattered body."

Taylor and I looked at one another in the eyes while he shook my limp right hand. There was something familiar about him—a kinship I couldn't quite place, but a comfort nonetheless.

Taylor enthusiastically showed us around the facility and spent the entire afternoon with Toots and me. He meticulously described each piece of equipment and how it could benefit my recovery. He then shared his passion for sport, admitting that he himself was a former soccer athlete and had experienced a career-ending ankle injury.

By the end of the day, I was on fire again. I was completely enthralled by Taylor and the center and knew in my heart that this was the way forward.

On a Mission

The slogan on my favorite red baseball hat said it all: "On a Mission." I think it was a surfing or snowboard company; I don't remember and forgot where I got the hat, but I do know that I loved it, and I wore it every day before the accident.

While I was still in the hospital, someone found that hat and brought it into my room. It hung in my view alongside the "Get Well" cards, posters, flowers, and balloons. I had not seen it since we'd come home from the hospital; it must have been boxed up and stored away with the rest of my room decor.

On the day that I nearly took my life at the pool, I rolled down the sidewalk toward our apartment with a tear-stained face. The words on that hat emerged in my mind.

I quietly repeated them to myself, louder and louder until I raged, "On a mission, On A Mission, I'M ON A FUCKING MISSION."

I howled at the sky, like Lieutenant Dan screaming at the storm atop the boat mast in the movie *Forrest Gump*. I didn't know what my mission was, but I was ready—ready to fight, suffer, and rise again. Those words became my rallying cry: "I'm on a mission!"

Toots found that hat and said it was apropos and symbolic for me to wear. The color red reflected my spirit and spurred the intensity I needed to focus on my recovery. We knew that nothing was going to work unless I did the work, so I wore it with true conviction.

During my first session with Taylor, I explained my hat and that I was on a mission to recover from my injury. I told him that the doctors thought that my mission was impossible and that I had a one-in-a-million chance of feeding myself.

"Well, let's just place an apostrophe between the I and the M and a space to make it 'I'm possible'!" Taylor replied. "We'll then focus on the ONE, and not the million."

"Ahhhhh yes, perfect!" I beamed.

Taylor and I quickly formed a special bond. Our friendship grew to become multidimensional. He was much more than my personal trainer. He became my educator and mentor, a pseudo psychiatrist, and a confidant for my most challenging days. I told him early on that other than my mother, he was the most important person in my life. We soon coined the phrase *Education + Motivation = Results*. That statement became our creed and underpinned all of our work together.

Besides Toots and Taylor, my inspiration was a vague yet impactful tale of a man who'd supposedly overcome paralysis. A physical therapist in the hospital told me this story, long before the days of social media. She showed me pixilated photos and news clippings of Patrick Rummerfield, a man who'd suffered a similar injury to mine back in the late 1970s. He had triumphantly persevered for more than twenty years to not only walk again but also compete in the Ironman Triathlon, drive race cars, and set a world land speed record in a battery-powered dragster at the legendary Bonneville Salt Flats in Utah. I could relate to this guy (especially his passion for racing) and his message: to never give up and to remove the concept of time.

I was accustomed to superficial injuries: break a bone, stabilize it, and then I could expect to cut the splint off eight to twelve weeks later as though nothing had happened. Eight to twelve weeks was a time frame, an expectation.

This was not the case with a spinal cord injury, and anyone who sets that expectation is doomed for a rude awakening.

I knew that my new path was indefinite and that removing a set time frame of recovery was going to help me to continue forward. I looked at Pat and thought, *Damn, he's still working hard two decades after his injury . . . and improving. I can do that!* His story solidified that understanding and became my example, the proverbial carrot for me to follow.

This was a massive perspective shift and an empowering way to keep me in the game day to day. I didn't need to hear anything more or track his continuing progress; I'd heard enough to set me in motion.

In therapy, I kept my head down and my eyes up—a fundamental racing rule that I applied to my recovery. In fact, I drew on many lessons I'd learned from racing a motorcycle:

- Don't look back . . . you're not going that way!
- When in doubt, gas it! Momentum is key.
- Seek incremental improvement each lap, because every second counts.
- Ask how to improve, not just why.
- The only difference between me and the fastest rider in the world is the six inches between my ears (this is one of my favorites).

Self-Induced Suffering (SIS)

Because spasticity ravaged my entire body, every single muscle fiber twanged with tension, and as I mentioned earlier in this story, my doctor suggested I subdue it with antispasmodic medication—a powerful muscle relaxer that would provide temporary relief but leave my body limp and even more immobile.

I preferred to use the involuntary contractions as an opportunity to connect to movements. The combination of my painted toes and muscle spasms allowed me the physical expression of visualization . . . connecting my mind to my muscles.

In fact, I rejected almost all the medication that was prescribed to me. My logic was that medication would mask signs and symptoms. I wanted to feel it all! Every single touch or the slightest twitch; every tickle, prick, pressure, or push. I wanted to distinguish between hot and cold, spasms, tissue tone, neuropathic pain, and muscle gains.

I called this approach self-induced suffering—suffering and relearning my body and its messaging on my terms. I suppose it's a bit masochistic, but I rested better knowing the source or cause of a sensation—and truth be told, I have a propensity for addiction. I knew that I could easily become dependent on any feel-good medication like painkillers or muscle relaxers. That really scared me! I had witnessed friends and family members succumb to substance abuse, and I knew full well that I wouldn't be any different.

"Create your own conditions, and the rain is just rain."
—AYRTON SENNA

There were times when I would writhe in pain, muscle spasms so harsh it felt like my bones were going to break and nerve pain so severe it was like my bare feet were held over hot coals. There were, and still are, many times throughout the day that I am in pain. My mind frequently wanders toward a desire for relief—maybe I'll just have one drink, take a pain pill, or smoke a joint. Again, these thoughts cause enough fear to make me abstain. I know that ultimately it wouldn't help me; in fact, it would more than likely hinder me and make things worse—a slippery slope I'm better off not treading.

Walking on Hands

Repetition, repetition, repetition . . . Taylor and I were on a roll, we were spending four to six hours a day, six days a week, committed to the grueling, monotonous process of influencing my recovery to regain movement.

"Let's take off your shoes for this exercise, Aaron," Taylor instructed. He removed my socks, exposing my bare feet and freshly painted toes. "Egads! Those are colorful, mate," he voiced with surprise. I told him the story of Arielle and her nail polish, and how I'd used the color of my toes for visualizing a reconnection. "Brilliant, Aaron!" He went on to explain the concept of neuroplasticity (the central nervous system's ability to rewire itself) and how important it was for me to visualize the exercises we were doing.

On occasion I would be the guinea pig for the kinesiology students at the center. Taylor and other instructors would use me for demonstration, or to illustrate their exercise science research. I was, at times, on full display for the class—a living cadaver of sorts.

I was happy to be the subject of study for the students. It kept things interesting and never allowed for the question, "Am I doing enough?" As the example, I'd exemplify an exercise with every ounce of energy and perform every rep and every set with maximum effort.

The majority of my therapy sessions consisted of hands-on assisted movements called proprioceptive neuromuscular facilitation (PNF) patterns, during which I'd lie flat on a table while a therapist moved my arms and legs through a full range of motion. Their instruction was for me to engage the movement, or push against their resistance to the best of my ability. I would think about the movement and visualize the colors and then explode with mental force—only to register a one, two, or maybe a three on the MRC strength scale.

*The Medical Research Council (MRC) grading system provides the following grades: zero—paralysis; one—only a trace or flicker of muscle contraction is seen or felt; two—muscle movement is possible with gravity eliminated; three—muscle movement is possible against gravity; four—muscle strength is reduced, but movement against resistance is possible; and five—normal strength.

Most of the muscles throughout my body had been compromised by the paralysis, and those that were firing were severely atrophied and unable to contract fully. To help activate the dormant tissues, I was often affixed to automated machinery that would stimulate muscle activity by electric shock and move my limbs around passively. This was called functional electrical stimulation, or FES.

Gradually over time the trace movements grew stronger and more coordinated. I continued to improve and graduate to more autonomous exercise equipment like the Flexorsizor, Easy Glider, Total Gym, and NuStep machine. I wore the grease out of that equipment—spending hours on it each day until I, and the machine, were thoroughly worn out. Quite literally, I had to bring a can of WD-40 lubricant into the center and spray the bearings just to stop the squeaking.

Roughly two years into my therapy at the center, I was standing upright between the parallel bars, staring in the mirror at my feet fighting to take a step when Taylor notified me: "Keep your head up, shoulders back, and your trunk erect . . ."

I paused, looked back over my left shoulder, and replied. "Would you like to know what it's like for me to relearn how to walk? It's like walking on your hands," I said earnestly. "Imagine the concentration, strength, endurance, balance, and coordination it takes to walk upside down on your hands. Now imagine walking down the hall, across the grass and up, and then down the stairs . . . on your hands. That's what I feel now, standing here, trying to make that happen."

There was constant dialogue in my head. I had to, and still have to, think about movement. I must consciously command my body with positive and sometimes bullish instructions to move. The more I learned from Taylor and the students, the more detailed my internal remarks became. The fundamentals of physics, and the laws of motion, leverage, and force enhanced my understanding of movement. I was as much, if not more, a student of my body than those formally enrolled.

During sessions I'd sometimes recall the words from a framed picture that hung in my bedroom. It read, "**There is in this world no greater force than the force of a man determined to rise.**" This quote inspired me, and it ultimately inspired a painting I created for a friend. I titled it *Rise Above*.

An Artistic Way

"Art is a way of survival."
—YOKO ONO

I was right-handed. Before my accident I could swing a baseball bat and throw a ball with either hand, but I always wrote with my right. I now had to learn to scribble with my impaired left hand. I called my writing chicken scratch because of the spastic marks I'd make. I could barely sign my name; my strained marks were different every time.

Bored and frustrated with skewed lines of letters and numbers, I began swooping and shading the paper with my pencil. My grip was light and awkward, shaky and spastic. The ever-frustrating left-handed smear was a major problem.

My new left hand / right brain exercise was creative and colorful. The paper became a kaleidoscope of color, more abstract than I'd originally intended.

Lynn Lupetti, a prolific artist and dear family friend from Carmel, was a lighthouse of support for Toots and me in those early days. She gifted me a set of paints, canvases, and a beautiful workstation to create from. To me, she is a modern alchemist of color and light and inspired me to begin experimenting with watercolor and gouache paint to illustrate my dreams and tell a story with art.

I'd dip the tip of the brush in paint and carefully raise it to the canvas. Usually a relaxing exercise, I'd sometimes be rudely interrupted by a muscle spasm that would jerk my arm across the paper and scar the landscape with a streak.

My impaired neural impulses would randomly interrupt an intended movement.

I'd think, exhale, make slow, delicate brushstrokes.

Instead, the signal that came down through my injured spinal cord into my arm was "Kablam!" Not a subtle brushstroke at all, but rather a rude jolt of neurochemical electricity . . . a shock of force—like the unkinking of a garden hose, unleashing pent-up water pressure into a powerful spray. Painting was a form of mental training; it was an active meditation and a practice of true patience.

My favorite piece depicts a man kneeling forward with the globe on top of his back. It symbolized the weight of the world upon his shoulders. In the background a faceless angel stands among rolling green hills, her wings outstretched and arm pointing him forward. In the center of the canvas, at the bottom of the scene, a winding road disappears into the horizon; the words *Rise Above* are signed in the lower right corner.

That painting was the first step in my creative process of redefining myself from paralysis. I was not a painter prior to my injury. I mean, I doodled here and there—mostly dirt bikes, waves, sunsets, or crude maps of future adventures. But now art had become a way to work with what worked—to create and achieve something tangible and to build my self-confidence. I was inspired.

Video Victories

Because recovery was a daunting and, in my case, an endless endeavor, improvements came slowly and in the form of tiny, sometimes unrecognizable, gains. I needed periodic wins to keep me engaged in the process long term.

Occupational therapy consisted mostly of mundane arts and crafts and electrical stimulation for improved fine-motor skills. Although picking up round pegs, paper clips, marbles, and Play-Doh were good for hand function, it was boring. Video games were reintroduced to me by a therapist and proved to be a real challenge to operate without adaptation, but it ultimately served as an enjoyable way to improve dexterity.

As a kid I played the occasional Nintendo video game when at a friend's house, because Toots didn't allow them at ours. I was never the one who stayed indoors in front of a TV after school; TV was reserved for sick days and movie nights.

But now I sat in front of a TV for many hours at a time, completely zoned out. The PlayStation video game console had a game controller with multiple buttons of different sizes and functions that I wanted to use without any modifications. So I convinced Toots that I needed my own game at home to practice with.

It took only a week or so for me to learn how to press the buttons firmly and quickly enough for motor-racing games—my hand therapy of choice. The virtual trophies brought temporary joy. Although I sat mostly paralyzed in my recliner, my mind was inside a helmet, racing once again.

I challenged anyone who'd play me and relished in victories. Those games helped level the playing field; gaming made me feel like I was improving, becoming stronger and good at something again.

The Puzzle

At this point I felt inspired, steadfast with momentum, and moving forward. All the therapies and art were paying off, granting me a renewed sense of self. In fact, I could now, for the most part, bathe and dress myself and drive my own adapted car—a huge step toward independence!

All the proverbial puzzle pieces of my life were intact but scattered out before me—I had no idea who I was as a person, if not an athlete. I knew that I wasn't going back to the life that was (a motocrosser) and that I was looking forward—my future seemed wide open, but unclear.

I began to use the term *recovering quadriplegic* rather than the orthodox complete/incomplete clinical nomenclature. To me this term felt open-ended, as though I was pursuing a possible outcome rather than the probable one the doctors gave.

"It all depends on me—I am responsible for the pieces of my puzzle—to put them together in order to see the big picture."

And because I still felt like an athlete, albeit an injured one, I'd just stay the course and make rehabilitation a lifestyle. This way of thinking allowed me to commit to a new, reimagined version of myself—a slow reassembling, one piece at a time—rebuilding and redefining who I was and what I stood for.

What I was to become was born from commitment . . . the process was the progress.

TO MY YOUNGER SELF

The breath and energy is rhythmic—in, out, in, out. I begin to *in-spire* with gratitude and acknowledge my existence by saying, "Thank you, body. I love you," and then exhaling. I am reminded of the miraculous gifts of time and love, and the privilege it is to be here and now. I imagine all the people, the places, and the things that bring me the most joy, and then I put pen to paper. I write out my thoughts, hopes, and dreams—my goals. This act is the first tangible step toward manifesting something from nothing—to make it real, it needs to be written, read and said.

Scan the QR code and head to
therebelliousrecovery.com/inspiration for
this part's complementary photo gallery.

BEGINNING

AWARENESS

SURRENDER

INSPIRATION

PART 5.1 # COMMITMENT

SERVE & SHARE

"Every flicker, every rep, every step, and every mile count. They add up and compound to more . . . much, much more."

Rising Above

I stared at my pale, skinny legs in the mirror, cycling around and around as the machine pedaled for me. The Flexorsizor, a bulky, silver metal, early iteration of an automated recumbent cycle was a must-do machine in my daily therapy sessions. Despite not having enough strength to initiate full-pedal movement myself, I could adjust the dial knob on the switch box to my left and control the speed at which the pedals turned automatically—which gave me the feeling of cycling again.

The words *Baker Rides Again* were printed across the back of my favorite T-shirt—a shirt that was made by a friend and given to me early in my recovery. I repeated those words in my mind as I pedaled left, right, left, right. My feet circled over and over, faster and faster. I would sit daily for an hour or more on this machine, begging my brain to connect with my body. I envisioned the colors again, my toes still painted, spinning spirals of energy up and down my body.

As I concluded a long meditative session and began to turn the dial down and then off, to my surprise, my legs kept cycling.

There was no power turning the pedals except my own, and in stunned silence I pointed in the mirror and smiled. Toots, the therapists, and other clients raised their hands and clapped; elated hugs followed from behind.

I knew in my heart that I was on the right track and had to keep the progress going. Thirty-six months into my recovery process I could stand and take tiny steps, and now spin pedals round—my brain was truly reconnecting to my body. It wasn't just a spasm; it was me really doing the work.

I had been attending the Center of Achievement for all that time but had never noticed the long-framed, two-seater bicycle that hung catawampus on the wall in a back office. Up to that point, the only frame of reference I had for a cycle of that type was a Doublemint chewing gum commercial with twin girls dressed alike, cycling together, and blowing double bubbles as they go.

Before my injury, you couldn't have paid me to ride a bike like that; nope, no way! My ego wouldn't do it.

It's funny how my ego took a back seat to desperation. Literally. My desire to ride again, to feel the wind in my hair and handlebars in my hands was so strong that it didn't matter I would be a rear-seat rider, pressed close to the pilot's sweaty derriere.

I quizzed Taylor about the tandem bicycle on the wall, asking if I could give it a go. Cautiously, he expressed concern about my safety and the liability for the center if, God forbid, an accident happened.

"Who do you suppose will ride the bike with you, Aaron?"

"You! Taylor."

"But, but, but . . ."

"You can pedal a bicycle, can't you, Taylor?"

"Well, yeah."

"Great! We've got this. Let's try it!"

Two therapy assistants finagled the bike from the wall and pushed it outside onto a wide walkway in the middle of the CSU Northridge campus. Taylor swung his leg over the bike seat and stood straight up with both legs straddling the bike frame and his feet flat on the ground. He held the handlebars with stiff arms and a tight grip.

Toots pushed my wheelchair over to the rear of the bike. She and another therapist hoisted my Gumby body up and onto the tiny rear seat. They strapped my feet to the flat pedals with Ace bandages and taped my hands loosely to the curved handlebars with white cloth athletic tape. The bike quivered beneath me; I felt Taylor's apprehension as Toots and the assistants held the bike upright and balanced.

I was nervous, too, but too excited to back out.

"Are you ready, Taylor?"

I counted: "Three . . . two . . . one . . ."

With a gentle push from behind by Toots, we coasted off and slowly began pedaling.

My feeble arms could barely brace against the handlebars, and because of my lack of torso strength, I tilted from side to side. I felt all my body weight press down onto the hard bike seat; I felt like a popsicle stick. I saw and felt my legs circle around, but I could not assist Taylor with any power. This experiment had the hallmarks of disaster, especially as we lost air in the front tire. A recovering quadriplegic and a fitness trainer attempt to ride a tandem bike? It sounded more like a news headline than a progress note on my therapy chart.

I heard Mimi, who'd been in town for the past week and who'd accompanied Toots and me during therapy sessions, holler, "Yahhh-hooooo, Aaron! Way to go!" as we slowly pedaled around the campus courtyard.

Five precarious minutes felt like an hour. The stress of staying upright and not crashing into a curb or a light pole was as exhausting as trying to turn the pedals over. I was light-headed; my blood pressure lowered with every pedal revolution. The handlebars twitched in Taylor's hands as the flattening front tire squished round, our legs slowly cycling in concert. We came to a sketchy stop, caught by the therapists and Toots just as my eyesight narrowed and my hearing muffled; thirty more seconds and I might have passed out.

"We can ride!" I gasped. "Toots, you're next!"

I signaled with my finger at the front seat as she unwrapped my hands from the handlebars.

"I'll ride with ya, buddy."

In Tandem

> "Teamwork makes the dream work."
> —JOHN MAXWELL

The first tandem bike ride with Taylor was a short, eye-opening experience. Although it was dangerous, it also showed me what was possible. It gave me a specific target to work toward within the scope of my recovery. I had more work to do if I was truly going to ride again safely.

Within three and a half years I had progressed from the FES electrical stimulator, to the Flexorsizor, to a NuStep recumbent stepper, to an upright stationary cycle. I could feel my neuropathways reconnecting. The continuous repetitive motion of pedaling allowed me to sit and send brain signals for hours on end. As Taylor had taught me, muscles and nerves that fire together, wire together. I was essentially rewiring my nervous system through cycling.

The smoldering, freshly laid blacktop in the parking lot at Lake Balboa Park north of Los Angeles, only ten miles from our house and physical therapy, was the initial testing ground for Toots and me on the tandem. We sat in the back of my SUV with the rear hatch up, staring at the long bike that lay on the ground in front of us. Although I continued to experience low blood pressure and needed to wear an abdominal binder and compressive stockings, I could stand upright with little assistance and some ankle bracing.

I stood from the car; Toots held my arm as I took a single step up and over the bike frame. She continued to hold my hand while I straddled the bike. She then circled around to the front and grabbed the handlebars, carefully lifting the bike up onto its wheels. I grabbed the handlebars with my left (stronger) hand while Toots swung her leg over the front seat. We stood there stiffly.

Starting off was the most precarious time on the bike. With no one there to hold the bike to balance us, we had to execute careful, synchronized choreography to prevent a spill. We both had to stand tall with our feet flat on the ground, straddling the bike frame with both hands securely on the handlebars.

With a firm squeeze of the brakes by Toots, I'd say, "Right pedal down"—which meant we had to shift our weight to our left legs and simultaneously spin the pedal cranks backward for the right pedal to be positioned in the vertical six-o'clock position. From there we could shimmy our right feet onto the pedal and into the pedal cage.

The cage was a modification to the pedals to secure our feet while in motion.

Finagling my foot in and out of the cage was a real hassle and took a lot of practice to master.

Once we both had our right feet firmly on the pedal, I would say, "Back pedal" again—which meant to spin the cranks backward a half revolution to the start stroke, about the two-o'clock position. As we balanced on our left and were primed with our right legs up and bent, we both exhaled and counted down from three. Just like I did as a motocrosser when sitting on the starting line, my elbows were up and ready for takeoff.

Three . . . two . . . one . . . push!

With an all-in-one motion, we pushed off from the ground with our left feet and stepped down on the pedal with our right, initiating just enough forward momentum to coast for ten to fifteen feet. While coasting, I had one shot to boost myself up onto my seat and catch the left pedal and cage with my left foot.

We'd modified our left pedals with a bungee cord by linking them together, cage side up, so we could place our feet on the pedal at the same time. This sequence had to be done in the span of about five seconds—otherwise we'd lose our momentum, come to a stop, and most likely crash.

The problem with stopping quickly was that I could not get my feet out of the cages and off the pedals fast enough to step onto the ground to help balance the bike. And Toots was not tall enough or strong enough to counterbalance all my weight leveraged in the rear. That was why every time we rode the tandem, whether it was for five minutes or fifty miles, we'd only start once and stop once.

Sometimes that didn't matter, because crashes happen. Our first mishap was in the Balboa parking lot during one of our first rides. We had circled the carless lot for barely over five minutes when my torso became weak and my arms buckled. I collapsed forward into Toots's back. She braced against me and turned us back toward our car, still coasting slowly.

I looked up and yelled, "Brakes!"

Toots had squeezed the handlebars so tightly that she couldn't release her grip fast enough to grab the brakes, and her arms were so stiff that she couldn't turn the bike either.

We careened into the rear of the car and crashed to the ground with our feet still secured to the pedals. We lay there in shock and confusion, traumatized but unhurt. We both shouted at each other in frustration and then laughed and cried.

"What the hell are we doing?" Toots said with remorse, fearing I could be injured further.

"We're OK," I assured her. "We just have to get better at communicating on this thing."

The tandem bike demanded our full attention. We had to cooperate and coordinate; otherwise, we'd end up a heap on the ground every time.

We continued to practice riding together, adding a few minutes to every ride. Five minutes turned into ten, then twenty, and then thirty. We rode consistently three to four days a week and began adding miles instead of minutes around the Lake Balboa bike path.

Toots was still the workhorse on the bike; she produced 70 percent of the power while I flailed behind, focused on sending brain signals to my legs. We'd go around and around the five-mile perimeter, practicing our gear shifts, braking, and steering. I barked orders from the back seat on how and when to maneuver. In my mind I was still a motorcycle racer, which I thought gave me the authority to direct our effort.

We became fairly savvy riders by the late summer of 2003; hundreds of laps had honed our skills. Nothing, though, prepared us for an unexpected encounter with a baby stroller.

It was one hundred degrees out. We had only half a mile until we reached the car and completed a grueling ten-mile (two lap) ride around the park. A woman ahead of us, jogging in the same direction while pushing a baby stroller, suddenly stopped and turned around with the carriage in hand. She swung the stroller directly into the middle of the narrow path. With an oncoming cyclist from the opposite direction, we had nowhere to go. Our front wheel smashed into the left side of the stroller, yanking it from the woman's grasp. We tumbled off the bike onto the cement.

I lay there shocked and fortunately unhurt while Toots jumped up to lift our wheel off the collapsed carriage. She stared into the empty stroller, confused. There wasn't a baby inside. We looked at each other, perplexed but relieved. I was furious at the woman for her reckless actions on a clearly marked bicycle path.

"This is a bike path!" I screamed. "What are you doing with a baby carriage out here? Thank God there wasn't a baby in there!"

The well-kept woman stood shocked and silent as her toddler ran out from behind a bush and across the bike path; another cyclist swerved around the oblivious child.

"Seriously, this path is dangerous," I scorned. "It's no place for kids to play!"

She just stood there with doe eyes and watched as Toots peeled me from the ground.

Don't Stop, Can't Stop!

It was now more than four years into my recovery, and I wanted more. I wanted to see numbers and objective data rather than someone's platitudes of progress. So I began compiling data from my rides with Toots to measure my progress.

The data motivated me and gave me measured marks of improvement, plateau, and sometimes even regression. Yes, *regression*. It became apparent early on that if I lapsed in my efforts or stopped therapy altogether due to illness, fatigue, or laziness, my body would revert back to paralysis so quickly that my head would spin. A common cold set me back months. I'd lose my physical abilities like someone loses their car keys. I hated this.

"Why do I lose my ability so quickly?" I asked Taylor.

"It's hard to say—spinal cord injury recovery is an emerging realm of study, and we're writing the new book as we go."

I asked my physical therapist, Roger, and other doctors and specialists the same question. All of them replied with a similar "I'm not sure" answer.

It was literally like flipping a light switch to my body on and off, and my emotions went with it. When I pushed hard, visualized, and focused my energy into movements, my body would slowly respond and improved in strength and coordination over time. And if I stopped, even if for only a few days, I'd lie heavily in place; it was like the light was switched off with no activation at all . . . all my functions stopped. I felt like hardened cement.

Every single day I awoke to an enigma. Will my body work today? Will it respond to my commands? Will it hold me up against gravity or buckle against my weight? The pendulum of uncertainty kept me on a razor's edge; some days I had the will to rise, and other days I was overwhelmed.

The bottom line was that I couldn't stop. Just like riding the tandem bike—once we got going and in motion, we had to keep up the momentum . . . otherwise, disaster.

I often said, "If I don't move forward, I die."

LA Marathon

Toots and I grew bored of lapping Lake Balboa five slow miles at a time. The same bike path and the same scenery in the sweltering heat made the once-enjoyable act downright miserable.

We had finally had enough when, while suffering another agonizing lap around the park, an elderly woman in sweatpants and flip-flops easily passed us while pedaling a rusty old beach cruiser.

"Awwwwwerrrrr!" I grunted from the back. "No way! Come on! Really?"

Toots and I were pushing the pedals as hard as we could, but still slugged along at ten miles per hour.

We didn't want to give up; we just wanted to improve and get faster, but we felt as though we'd hit a plateau and were just riding around in circles . . . literally.

Due to our regular visits to Valley Bikes, our local bike shop in Chatsworth, California, for bike maintenance and gear, Bob the owner took interest in our backstory and introduced us to Vince from KHS Bicycles. Vince became a huge supporter and our first sponsor.

Bob then introduced us to former Tour de France cyclist turned coach Roy Knickman. Roy lived nearby, which really helped. Intrigued by our desire to improve on the bike, Roy took us on as clients. He treated us no differently from any of his other athletes and designed an intense training plan for us to follow. Roy suggested we set a specific goal, like a race or charity ride.

"For an athlete to function properly, he must be intent. There has to be a definite purpose and goal if you are to progress. If you are not intent about what you are doing, you aren't able to resist the temptation to do something else that might be more fun at the moment."
—JOHN WOODEN

Soon after, while en route to therapy at the Center of Achievement, I noticed a billboard that advertised the Los Angeles Marathon—a 26.2-mile charity ride. Every March, thousands of cyclists converge onto the streets of downtown Los Angeles.

"It's only 26.2 miles," Toots said. "If we train for it with Roy, I think we can do it! Wouldn't it be fun to ride through downtown LA?"

"Oh yeah!" I agreed.

With Roy guiding us, we had only four months to train and progress from an average of ten miles per ride to an intimidating twenty-six miles.

We needed new training grounds that provided hills and

turns—conditions and technical riding that could prepare us for the marathon.

Naively, I opened the Thomas Guide paper map and guessed which roads near us would be safe and ridable in lieu of Lake Balboa Park. We found ourselves alongside some very precarious motorways and sometimes deep in secluded canyons and citrus fields, far away from any aid or alternate route out of the situation.

Rain or shine, sleet or heat, we rode with fervor.

Our favorite route was along the Pacific Ocean where sheer cliffs met the sea. We pedaled up and down the Pacific Coast Highway (PCH 1) from Malibu to Ventura County and back, three days a week.

The iconic coast road was a scenic training ground, with canyon offshoots where the hot asphalt climbed and wound up the Santa Monica Mountains. Those roads reminded us of when Toots had lived in Malibu high up Coral Canyon on a steep, windy road I used to lunge down on my skateboard. While riding, we told each other stories about those times and how much fun we'd had.

The roads were no joke, though. Sports car drivers and motorcyclists were fast, and the tourists and lookie-loos were distracted by the view. Often, a peloton of professional cyclists and their support teams passed us. They'd zoom by us, holler, and wave. Yet there we were, a recovering quadriplegic and his mom, laboring against the pedals, sweating in the sun, cussing at the incline, and spitting our way down the road.

Trancas Country Market, at the farthest west end of Malibu, was our start and end point for every ride. My SUV was our salvation from the sun and our place of rest with lunch or snacks after our ride.

Soft cheddar cheese slices unwrapped from car-heated tinfoil and honeycrisp apple slices were a coveted end-of-ride snack. On occasion, we indulged in a market-deli sandwich with a side of pickle spears, kettle chips, and a Coke.

On Saturdays, a local pit master brought his mobile barbecue grill into the parking lot and served up smoked meats and sides . . . the scent of which wafted in the air along the coastline and inspired our last few weary miles back to the car and his cooking.

These were the days that hardened us—long, undulating miles with coastal headwinds among heavy traffic and road laws. Wednesdays were trash days—large blue and green trash cans and recycling bins obstructed the shoulder lane and had to be cautiously navigated around, as well as trash trucks and parked cars.

By the time we lined up on West Jefferson Boulevard in front of the University of Southern California campus at 4:00 a.m. with thousands of other cyclists for the LA Marathon, we were prepared . . . or so we thought. We felt confident in our ability to start and stop the tandem and pedal twenty-plus miles in a single ride; however, we'd always done it alone, without anyone around, and never among a sea of people.

We sat along the curb amid thousands of anxious riders hopped up on coffee and adrenaline, our game plan all but thrown out the window. We were deer in headlights about to throw ourselves onto the road in a way we were not expecting or prepared for.

First of all, it was still dark out. We'd never ridden in the dark, and we didn't have any lights. It was freezing cold. Both Toots and I were bundled up in long-sleeved Lycra, gloves, beanies, and goggles—way more layers of clothing than we'd ever cycled in before.

"What if I have to pee?" I asked Toots.

I'd recently stopped wearing a leg bag while riding and quickly realized that my timing was terrible and wished I had worn one.

I tried to remain calm and focused, but I was stressed. I saw Toots gripping the handlebars so tightly that her knuckles were white.

"We've got this," I reminded her, moments before we pushed off with the others.

The start gun sounded at the end of our count: three . . . two . . . one!

"Hey, watch out!"

"Whoaaa!"

"Get out the way!"

Riders yelled and swerved all around us as we attempted our start sequence. Our long tandem twitched and swerved slowly, with Toots grappling the handlebar and brakes. We dodged riders that would start and then stop and put their feet down, causing a traffic jam. We couldn't stop, at least not quickly, without falling over. Once we got the bike rolling, we had to keep it rolling. Part of our problem was that nobody knew we had a special circumstance. I don't think anyone would have suspected me as having a spinal cord injury. Thus, no one had any patience or consideration for our slow, wide load. We had to muscle our way through the chaos to keep our momentum up to prevent falling over and crashing. Both of our mindsets changed at the same time as we shifted gears, clicking over from scared, defensive riders into aggressive, competitive cyclists.

Toots leaned forward in an attack position, grunting forcefully as she pushed the pedals around. I stayed upright, scouting the road ahead, calling out cues to follow.

Rider left . . . shift up . . . brake . . . pedal down . . . coast . . . water.

These simple cues kept us in sync with each other as we threaded our way through droves of casual cruisers, up and down unseen streets in downtown Los Angeles.

The miles seemed to tick by quickly as my perception of time and distance was skewed by the adrenaline that kept us oscillating between fight and flight.

We pedaled east toward the finish line and witnessed the sunrise amid a large convivial crowd that lined the final stretch. There was loud music playing.

"We are LA!" the crowd sang as we crossed under the checkered archway.

I pumped my fist and tapped Toots on the back.

"We did it, Toots!" I panted, my lips dry and stuck to my teeth.

We bypassed the stopped line of riders waiting for their medals and continued circling the USC campus looking for a safe, open area to stop and dismount. We laid the bike down and collapsed onto a bench, exhausted. We looked at each other and hugged.

"Whoa! What a ride. I can't believe we finished and didn't crash." Toots exhaled.

"No kidding! That was intense. Nice riding, Toots!" I stretched out along the bench to lie flat and propped up my feet, my blood pressure dropping fast. I closed my eyes and remembered all the hours I'd spent on the Flexorsizor, sitting in front of the mirror, watching my paralyzed legs pedal round. I uttered, "We make one helluva team, Toots. Thank you for your commitment and never leaving my side."

INTERLUDE

A Needed Break

I was exhausted; I felt physically and mentally overworked. I'd spent nearly five years with my proverbial blinders on in a self-imposed, isolated bubble. My life revolved around rehab, a cycling schedule, and the goals I'd set; I needed a break.

I dialed my friend Brian Cernius, who at the time lived in Las Vegas. He and I shared a brotherly connection; I was older by four years. We loved motorcycling, from which we both had suffered spinal cord injuries at a young age. From a wheelchair, Brian led a remarkably independent life. By the age of twenty-one, he'd amassed his own palatial home, a Ferrari, and a garage full of off-road vehicles. He was self-made with little education and was an immense inspiration to me.

"Hey, B! I'm heading your way tomorrow," I said on the call.

"Come on up. Your room is clean. Diesel [his English bulldog] hasn't slept on your bed in a while," Brian replied with a laugh.

The desolate drive through the desert north to Nevada set the tone for my trip. The windows were down, and the music was up; the hot desert air filled me with a feeling of independence. That feeling was what I'd been working toward the entire time since my accident. It had been five years since I'd driven solo, pumped my own gas, or hauled my own luggage . . . I was on the road again by myself and I loved it!

I'd been there only a few days when we made an impromptu plan to visit Hawaii, where Brian's family had a villa on the island of Maui. I was still in rebellion against the wheelchair and made a risky decision to leave it behind and travel only with the use of my cane. Brian and I negotiated our way through the airport; Brian in his chair and me holding our bags, ushered by the airport's skycap golf cart.

I walked slowly down the narrow aisle of the airplane and grabbed the window seat, pressing my nose to the window glass as we lifted off. We were giddy with excitement and cracked jokes, drank Cokes, and gobbled packets of sweetened peanuts while planning our week's sojourn.

The warm island air wafted over me as we exited the terminal, sparking memories of my family travels when I was younger.

Wow, I thought, *I'm traveling again.*

Like a dry sponge, I absorbed the fragrant scent of jungle flowers and moist sea air, taking every breath deeper and deeper. Feeling nostalgic, I shared with Brian how much it meant for me to be independent and traveling.

"I can't believe we're actually in Maui! Can't you smell it?"

"Ha ha . . . smell what, dude?" Brian sniggered.

"Freedommm!" I howled, standing curbside while waiting for Brian's dad to collect us.

Not one to show much emotion, he smirked and said, "You want freedom? Let's get a rental Jeep. Can you drive a stick shift?"

"Ha, I could before my injury. Yeah, let's try it!"

The only other vehicles I had driven since my accident were a heavily adapted driver's training van with hand controls and my Ford Explorer, modified with a left-foot accelerator pedal and steering knob.

Phil, Brian's dad, rented a topless, rusty blue Jeep for us. Brian and I waited out of the sight of the rental car manager.

"You're sure you've got this?" Brian asked from the passenger seat while I heaved his wheelchair up and over the roll bar and into the open back seat.

"We'll see, won't we?" I said with a chuckle.

I pressed the clutch pedal with my stronger left foot.

"It won't be pretty, but I think we can do it," I added. "I'll work the pedals and the steering wheel if you pull the gear shift."

"Ohhh man, this'll be good," Brian said with a laugh, while he tugged the shift lever into reverse.

I eased off the clutch . . . and the Jeep jerked backward and then stopped.

We were hysterical. Our eyes teared from laughter; my cheeks hurt from smiling.

"Dude, dude; come on, stop, dude!" Brian cried while laughing.

Like a couple of mischievous schoolboys giddy and gleeful, we tag-teamed the task of driving the Jeep. I pushed in the clutch while Brian shifted into third gear; we sped up and cruised along the waterfront on Maui's eastside. The wind blew through the windowless cab; Bob Marley blared through the speakers.

"Wooohooo!" I hollered.

We sang the words to "Jammin'" at the top of our lungs!

It was a perfect song for two paralyzed guys jamming gears on a road to nowhere.

The next day we loaded the Jeep with fresh island fruits and homemade bread from a farmers' market and set off for the black sand beach on the opposite side of the island. We stopped to snorkel at Mile Marker 14, notorious for tiger sharks and sea turtles. We then drove to the summit of the Haleakalā Volcano for lunch and the view. We circumnavigated the island and trespassed beyond closed roads and lava fields in the Jeep, our getaway car. We were young and reckless, rebelling against the rules and our wheelchairs. We were carefree and felt free; it was a *Lord of the Flies*-like adventure, just the two of us. I helped Brian and he helped me. We complemented our different abilities—I was the legs and he was the arms. Together we solved problems and found ways to enjoy the journey despite our limitations. We transformed our adversity into an adventure!

It was the trip of a lifetime—my first real sense of freedom and a taste of independence like never before.

Talk the Walk

Because of our unique mother-and-son cycling successes on the tandem, the City of Los Angeles awarded Toots and me with a plaque of recognition followed by a newspaper article. Taylor asked if we'd be willing to accompany him on stage for a presentation that he was giving at a health-and-fitness industry conference. He wanted us to share our client and mother perspectives on recovery from injury. What the three of us ended up creating and rehearsing was a lengthy keynote presentation called "The Man Inside the Helmet."

We had a special dynamic, the three of us. Taylor spoke clinically about exercise science and the biomechanics of human movement and how, under the right circumstances, the body can do remarkable things. I spoke from my perspective as an injured athlete and how I do what I do and what I feel in the process. Toots shared her vital role as a facilitator, earning the all-encompassing moniker "Motherpist"—mother and therapist.

Our talks were often given to audiences of doctors, scientists, researchers, and therapists during a time when recovery from a spinal cord injury like mine was rare and not fully understood. Our story, much like Pat Rummerfield's, was anomalous; we shared a process and a commitment to healing that the antiquated textbooks did not speak about. We eventually found ourselves on a main stage in San Diego, accepting the Met-Rx World's Best Personal Trainer and Client Award for Outstanding Transformation.

Toots and I began to share our story on our own, speaking with newly injured patients as well as their families, doctors, and therapists. We spoke with passion about prognosis and the importance of planting seeds of hope and possibility early in one's recovery. We were highly sensitive not to misconstrue our message with false hope, as we lived the fragile psychological roller coaster every day.

On stage we found a purpose as the spotlight exposed our greatest vulnerabilities; our story was a reflection for so many others. The authentic connections we made by sharing our struggles gave us meaning in an otherwise ambiguous cycle of pain and suffering. My process of recovery began to give me a whole new level of identity, and I became emboldened in my abilities.

One day, not long after the Met-Rx World event and completing another cycling marathon from Rosarito to Ensenada, Mexico, we were in front of a large audience.

I turned to Toots and blurted out the question, "Since we've ridden the tandem bicycle in these marathons and all over Southern California roads, why don't we just ride across the country like Forrest Gump?"

The audience gasped and then chuckled at the Forrest Gump reference, while Toots stared at me blankly. My declaration sat heavily in the room, causing an awkward silence.

I turned to the audience and stirred the energy with, "Why not? If we can ride 26.2 miles in less than two hours, we can surely ride three thousand miles in three months."

Heads tilted—but again, crickets.

BEGINNING

AWARENESS

SURRENDER

INSPIRATION

PART 5.2 # COMMITMENT

SERVE & SHARE

"What lies behind us, and what lies before us are
but tiny matters compared to what lies within us."
—RALPH WALDO EMERSON

The Rise Above Tour

I could see my life on the road. The vision was clear in my mind—not necessarily how I was going to pedal three thousand miles, but east. I wanted to pedal east. Like driving a car at night, all I needed was to see as far ahead as my headlights. The adventure, however, was going to take some serious planning.

> **"A goal without a plan is just a wish."**
> —Antoine de Saint-Exupéry

I drew upon my motorcycle-racing background and knew that we were going to need sponsors to finance a motor home with a trailer, extra equipment, teammates, logistics . . . and, and, and . . . life on the road. The cross-country bicycle ride was going to cover thousands of miles and last for months, and important basic needs had to be met. I was going to need a comfy bed, an accessible bathroom and shower, and access to good food throughout the day no matter where we were. Especially since most of the tour route would be well off the beaten path, along back roads and rural countryside areas where amenities were few and far between.

Before we actually acquired an RV, Toots and I played a little game while training along PCH.

Any time a nice RV passed us, we yelled, "Hey! Wait up!"

We were jokingly implying that it was our motor home and it would pull over and wait for us up the road. This was our way of visualizing the future, imagining what we wanted and saying it out loud to each other.

The Route

I began with a map. I searched the internet for the best cycling routes and found a fantastic resource called AdventureCycling.org. The website was a gold mine of information, with multiple routes west to east and north to south. The individual maps they provided were made by cyclists for cyclists with all the pertinent information for transcontinental touring, such as safe, quiet roads away from interstate highways, food markets, bike shops, and campgrounds along the way. The maps provided detailed information about climate history during different times of year, elevation change and topography data, and the flora and fauna to be expected in different states.

I selected the shortest, easiest, and most plausible route to go west to east, called the Southern Tier. It totaled 3,182 miles beginning at Dog Beach, San Diego; traversing the southernmost parts of the United States across California, Arizona, New Mexico, Texas, Louisiana, Mississippi, and Alabama; and ending in the sand in St. Augustine, Florida.

These maps lit my bulb even brighter and allowed me to illustrate my vision in a sponsorship proposal.

The Team

With the route framework in place and sponsorship proposals in the mail, I made a list of all things I'd potentially need—including the team. Toots and I were bold but not bold enough to think we could go at it alone. We knew we needed a solid group of trusted friends and family members to help make this happen. I envisioned it much like a motocross race team in the way we would travel the country with equipment and personnel—a process with which I was already familiar; just something I hadn't done with so much at stake.

Although Toots and I had been pedaling together for five years, we knew it would take an entire team of riders to get across the country. So Toots's main role became tour facilitator. She organized the public speaking schedule, my sponsorship appearances, and other logistics. She would fly to specific cities to ride with me.

To fill her big shoes, or should I say *seat*, my first call was to Adam Zerbe. Because he'd stayed with us and helped care for me when first discharged from the hospital, he already knew my needs and daily routine. His strength and cycling prowess and passion for adventure made this call a no-brainer.

"Hey, Zerbler!" I said on the call.

Our boyhood lingo picked up right where we'd left off, a surf/skateboard kind of tone.

"Do you have any plans for the summer?" I asked cheekily.

"Just working the surf shop and catching waves. Why? What are you scheming?"

Adam is always up for a good time, so I led with, "How would you like to ride beach to beach across the country?"

"What the . . . you mean coast to coast? The entire United States?"

"Yeah. The whole shebang—three thousand–plus miles!"

"Sheeesh!"

"Yeah, man. You and me on a tandem bike with a team of friends."

I heard the wheels in his brain spinning.

"How do you plan to make this happen?" Adam quizzed.

"Well, if you say yes, then we start riding together."

I then explained my "race team" approach and how I would reach out to specific companies for sponsorship.

"I'm in," Adam said with the boyish excitement I fondly recalled from our childhood.

"Sweet," I replied. "Now let's see if Bice is on board."

Adam Bice from Malibu was my guy—he was exceptional in my mind and someone I could always count on.

The timing of my proposition was perfect for him, and without hesitation Bice signed on with a "Hell yes!"

These two Adams played a vital role as my teammates aboard the tandem. They were going to take over Toots's hard-earned seat and trade off and on throughout the tour.

My vision slowly became a reality as one by one my friends signed on to join the tour. Adam Bice and Adam Zerbe were my tandem teammates. Ben Marius, another friend from Malibu, served as a support rider; Miles McBreen, a friend of Zerbe's, was our photographer and a helping hand; and a beautiful young empath named Hollyn Thompson, who happened to be my undercover crush, served as our nutrition specialist—a fancy title for cook, the one who fed all the hungry boys . . . and who would also, later, be at the center of a terrible quarrel between Zerbe and me.

The Setup

Two months prior to our scheduled start date of June 10, 2007, and eight years into my recovery, Zerbe moved down from Carmel and into our house in Santa Clarita to begin training with me. We first visited my former cycling coach, Roy Knickman, to help us fit both Adams to the tandem, because it had been originally fitted for Toots—five foot five, 120 pounds.

Roy changed everything on the bike—the handlebars and the seat, the seat post and the pedals; these modifications fit both guys and allowed for long, comfortable miles in the saddle.

Roy's training prescription was more of what Toots and I were accustomed to, but the Adams had not yet done this type of training. Roy wanted us to enter charity events and log as many miles together as possible on PCH and steep canyon roads.

The Bus

The clock was ticking . . . we had only two weeks before the start date and had the team locked in and our primary sponsors on board, but we still had not secured a support vehicle.

I knew exactly what I was looking for. I had already mocked up an illustration on my computer the year before. I'd dreamed about the perfect traveling rig with colorful graphics and sponsor logos, like a rock band's tour bus. I could see it in my mind so clearly that no ordinary RV would do. However, time was of the essence, and I was beginning to get a little desperate. I even considered camping some of the way.

Forty-five minutes north of Los Angeles on the outskirts of a town called Lancaster was Rexhall Motor Coaches, a lesser-known motor home company on the verge of going out of business. I was optimistic about a used coach I had found online, which was the reason for our visit to their headquarters. The sun-faded gray-and-white family motor home was quite underwhelming and riskier than it was worth. The tires were dry and cracked, the refrigerator didn't work, and the engine had more miles than advertised. We had to keep looking. I'd dragged Toots, Zerbe, my sister, and my dad out to the desert to see this rig, and it turned out to be a dud. The sales manager could tell we were disheartened and offered up a Hail Mary.

"Since y'all came all this way, come round back," the manager said. "I've got one that y'all probably won't like, but you may as well see it anyway; it's in your price range."

All of us crammed onto a dilapidated golf cart with our arms and legs hanging off as we rounded the warehouse toward the back lot. There it sat—forty feet of black, gray, orange, and chrome, the once-famed Harley-Davidson executive tour bus. It was a spitting image of the one in my dream, the one that I'd mocked up with my computer software.

"Holy moly, that's it!" I yelled as we pulled up.

We gazed at its glory and walked around the outside, kicking its tires and touching the paint.

"Sold," I said.

"But you haven't seen the inside and all of its features," the manager responded.

I already knew this was the one; he didn't have to convince me one bit.

We boarded the beauty, and I immediately sat down in the black pleather captain's chair behind the wheel. I blew the horn, and everyone jumped.

"We're hitting the road!" I hollered.

We sat in a state of shock and awe at the perfection of our find.

For about thirty minutes we played and lay on the beds, couches, and fresh carpeted floor. I flipped on the gas fireplace and rested there, even though it was ninety-five degrees outside.

This thing had two slide-out walls that nearly doubled the living space when parked. It had a dishwasher, double-door refrigerator, walk-in shower, washer and dryer, two TVs, and a king-size bed in the main bedroom.

"Where do we sign?" I asked.

Honnk, honnk!

I sounded the horn again as I turned out of the parking lot and onto the frontage road. I sat sidesaddle in the driver's seat, gripping the oversize steering wheel while operating the two right-side accelerator and brake pedals with my stronger left foot. I'm sure the manager was surprised to see that I was the one driving the rig off the lot. After all, we had just spent the last four hours with the sales team talking about my spinal cord injury, paralysis, and all my limitations. I'd never mentioned I could drive.

I think I blew the horn one hundred times on the drive home; I just couldn't contain myself. The final big piece to the tour plan was complete, with only six days to go. All I had to do was to have the bus wrapped with our sponsor logos.

The Story Brand

The tour needed a title, a story I could tell to sponsors. I used the phrase "Rise Above" often in the gym, on the bike, and even in my art—like in the Genesis painting I'd gifted my friend Jake, who subsequently tattooed "Rise Above" on his back. The more I thought about it, the more obvious it became. The Rise Above Tour had a ring to it, and with a phoenix as our logo, it symbolized my journey up and out of the ashes of injury.

I drove the bus straight to the decal shop not far from our house and parked out front, even though they were closed.

There's no sense in sleeping at home, I thought.

I was already at home; the bus was more comfortable and easier for me than our two-story town house.

I flipped on the diesel generator for electrical power, ordered a pizza, and turned on a movie. I slept like a baby.

The next day the decal crew got to work and quickly adorned the exterior sides with NASCAR-style stickers—our Rise Above Tour logos, phoenix and all.

June 9

T-minus twelve hours and we were parked at the local Camping World, next door to a Super Walmart. The rig was alive with activity; the gas generator hummed, powering all the lights inside and out. Every cupboard and compartment door was open, fully stocked and organized with supplies. The music was pumping while busy bodies crawled in and out, up and down, over and under every nook and cranny of our new home on wheels.

Adam Bice and Ben Marius showed up with bags and bikes in hand. I blew the horn again.

"All aboard, fellas!" I hollered as I sat inside, organizing the resources cabinet above the left side of the driver's compartment. This held the most important documents for the road: bus operations manual, repair resources, proof of insurance, maps, etc.

With that much action so late at night, our corner of the dark parking lot must have looked like a misplaced campground party. I kept time and encouraged the team to wrap up by midnight so we could get enough sleep for our big send-off ride in San Diego the following day.

With bodies still lying on the floor and on foldout beds in the living room, I fired up the diesel engine. The rig roared to life, waking the boys and newly added teammate Miles—the photographer. We were soon southbound for San Diego; Dog Beach was our starting point.

D-Day

My memory of that day is foggy. I know I drove the bus there and parked it among one hundred or so people. Friends, friends of friends, family members and their friends, and strangers curious about our commotion were all around the bus, lying on the grassy area in the parking lot and strewn across the beach . . . walking dogs, of course. The energy was electric, and things were happening quickly.

Before I got swept up in the action, I remember lying in the back bedroom by myself, reflecting on how far I'd come. Eight years earlier I had been lying in a hospital bed paralyzed from the chin down, and now I was about to embark on an epic bicycle journey. Tears filled my eyes with pride and gratitude as I chuckled to myself about a memory of a morphine-induced dream I'd had in the hospital. The dream was about me having long, funky hair and shaved legs, wearing skimpy spandex cyclist shorts while pedaling around the world. Besides the long hair, that dream was now my reality, and I laughed.

Just then Zerbe burst into the bedroom and gave me a titty twister, hootin', "Come on, Bake. Let's get it on! Everyone is waiting for you."

The front of the bus was packed full of excited people; everyone was talking to each other and dancing to the music. I emerged from the back and started fist-pumping, high-fiving, and hugging everyone.

Hollyn finally arrived. She bounded onto the bus with a wide smile and tackled me in the hallway, causing us both to stumble backward onto the bed. She was a stunning beauty with long blonde hair, starlit eyes, and a booming personality; she was a dear platonic friend, but she also happened to make my heart pound and knees weak. I kept those feeling to myself, though, because for now she was the welcome final member of our team and was responsible for managing the bus, preparing our daily meals, and generally keeping us organized while on the road.

It was 9:50 a.m. and we all gathered around the table in the living room. We looked over our route map one last time and coordinated our first stop with my dad, who had signed on as the bus driver (a role he shared with five others who came and went along the way) for the first 432 miles to Tempe, Arizona.

We put our hands together in the middle of the table to say a little prayer, then gave the chant, "One . . . two . . . three . . . Rise Above!"

Zerbe held my hand as I carefully stepped over the tandem bike frame while Toots looked on. I can only imagine the emotions she felt from not being the one to ride with me on this day. She and I had spent so many long hours on the road together, pedaling for no other purpose than to progress. Well, this was the progress, and I know she knew that.

Bice and Ben cleared the way for Zerbe and me to count off our start sequence—three . . . two . . . one . . . push!

We were off, swerving to avoid the crowd and other riders in our send-off group. We rode slowly through the parking lot over to the trailhead, fist-pumping and howling with our entourage along the way. The river mouth bike path followed the water wash east for fifteen miles along Highway 8, our predetermined route to the base of the Cuyamaca Mountains and a Walmart for our first night's stay.

A Walmart parking lot, a Camping World parking lot, a KOA campground, or an RV park were each day's destination. These places ensured us safety and resources and were large enough to legally park the bus and the vehicle following us—my Jeep driven by our photographer, Miles. The campgrounds and RV parks allowed us to hook up to power as well as water and sewer . . . great luxuries when you've gone a few days without them.

Still buzzing, we stayed up late and recounted the day, the route, and what was to come. We barely slept. The following day, a few friends who had followed in their cars joined us as we began to climb up into the mountains toward the Alpine Summit.

Our plan was to pedal thirty to sixty miles every day. The bus would leapfrog ahead of us about three to five miles at a time, stopping to assist us with water, snacks, and maintenance, if needed. What we didn't account for was that the first thirty miles was a steep climb from sea level to over two thousand feet! I was naive and overzealous, because by the time we reached the Alpine Summit we were all completely exhausted. The excitement quickly wore off as we began to feel the effects of hard back-to-back rides . . . the challenge of real tour cycling.

By the fifth day we were way off pace and behind schedule; we were barely one hundred miles in, slugging our way up the mountain to the high plateau east of San Diego. Our energy lifted as we shifted our bikes into high gear to head down the steep, windy road to the desert below.

"Yewwww!" I hollered from the back seat, with Zerbe tucked low over the handlebars.

Peeking over his shoulder, I saw the speedometer clocked at forty-eight miles per hour and the temperature was seventy-eight degrees. We were hauling ass!

All was well when we began our descent . . . until we were smacked in the face by an alarming desert heat. Like opening the oven door, the temperature jumped thirty degrees to 110 in the span of five miles.

What Are We in For?

Our caravan ground to a halt in Jacumba Hot Springs.

"Are we nuts?" Bice said, concerned.

"Damn, it's hot," Ben yelled.

None of us had expected that kind of heat. But, really, what did we expect? It was the middle of June, and we were riding across the southernmost part of the United States. I guess it was a good thing that we were a bit naive . . . because if we'd known this part of the route would have been this hot, none of us would have signed up.

We couldn't stay stopped long; heat radiated from the asphalt and intensified the lack of shade. With the breeze, the temperature would be about 103 degrees . . . so we were better off moving.

The tour quickly became a game of survival. Dad kept the bus right behind us with the hazard flashers on as we traversed along the Mexico-California border; it was fifty miles to the nearest town, Calexico.

As we pedaled on, my mind wandered. I thought about the desperate days after the accident and the time Toots found herself jailed in Calexico and lying facedown in the ditch along the road. *Those were times of survival*, I thought. If we'd endured that misery, then the heat that we were complaining about was no sweat.

That was my biggest problem, though—I can't sweat! I am unable to thermoregulate my body's temperature to cool myself down. This was a major issue when dealing with heat. If my internal temperature rose above ninety-nine degrees, then I would become incredibly sick. Aside from heatstroke, it could trigger what is known as autonomic dysreflexia, a condition where my nervous system sends chaotic signals that cause dramatic fluctuations of blood pressure and heart rate. I could potentially suffer a stroke or, even worse, death.

While I'd trained for this during rehab, I hadn't ridden so many back-to-back days in this kind of heat. My body revolted but still functioned enough to pedal . . . so we continued. Smoldering blacktop tar stuck to our tires and slung up the back side of my jersey; the asphalt was hot enough, I'm sure, to fry an egg.

While in the desert, my favorite time of the day was dusk . . . when the sun sat low amid the sand dunes and the barren wasteland emerged as magical. The four of us pedaled into the night through Glamis and across the Imperial Sand Dune Wilderness. Silhouettes of windswept dunes lit by a full moon surrounded us; the paved road was visible without the need for headlights. We were modern cowboys atop modern steeds in an old land that was a sea a long time ago. We rode on.

River Shave

Our first two-day reprieve from the scorched sandscape was at the border of California and Arizona in an RV campground along the

Colorado River in Ehrenberg. There we rested, laundered clothes, and restocked food, water, and ice from the local grocer. I sat in a lawn chair in the shallow water at the edge of the river and shaved my legs, while Hollyn giggled at me.

"Here, you're next," I said with a laugh and handed her the razor. She lathered her legs, shaved, and bathed in the river with me.

Father's Day Spandex

We were a day's ride outside of Phoenix, and it was Father's Day. To celebrate, I asked Dad, who'd been driving the bus, if he'd ride the tandem with me for a few miles. He squeezed into my extra pair of spandex shorts and jersey that matched mine and swung his leg over the bike. Both Adams coached him on how to control the tandem, since he hadn't ridden a bike like that before. We got going in the right direction, only to be stopped a half mile later when the road dead-ended. We circled back.

"Dad, I love you, and happy Father's Day, but let's wrap this up," I said.

We had too far to go and too little time to be lollygagging around, as we had scheduled events in Phoenix early the next day.

The Rise Above Cocktail

We rolled into the news station like rock stars and filed out of the bus one at a time up to an awaiting news anchor with a microphone. We each gave a live interview and invited locals to join us later that evening at an event in Scottsdale, where a gracious restaurateur named Natasha opened her wine bar and tasting room up to us for a night of celebration and fundraising; she even dedicated a signature cocktail to us called "Rise Above." We drank, mingled, and enjoyed the much-needed time off the road, waking up the next day parked in the driveway of my Aunt Wendy and Uncle Joe's house.

We spent two days washing and restocking the bus, organizing things, resting, swimming, and sunbathing . . . all in preparation for another few hundred miles across southern Arizona.

Toots Aboard

We hit Tucson and headed straight toward the airport to pick up Toots. She had flown in to join us for the route through New Mexico to El Paso, Texas.

Toots and I were again united on the bike and rode our way through old Apache Indian land littered with towering saguaro cacti and slated red rock. The road thrusted upward, and Zerbe returned to the front of the bike. We pedaled painfully slowly up toward the great Continental Divide in the Gila National Forest. The windy road was so steep that Zerbe's knee succumbed to his effort; it was enough of an injury to leave him writhing in pain and have him retire the front seat to Bice.

At nearly five thousand feet, the southwestern New Mexico mountains were a window to the stars . . . the night sky a black blanket with holes punched through it. We camped near an observatory and gazed across the cosmos, seeing too many shooting stars to count.

With Bice at the helm, we blitzed through Silver City and across to Las Cruces. We logged some of our longest days in the saddle, sixty-plus miles at a time. So long that my two big toenails turned black and blue from the intensity. During periodic rest stops along the road's edge, I sat on a frozen bag of corn in an attempt to subdue the swelling between my legs. The consecutive long, hot days were taking a toll on me. My usual padded cycling shorts were not enough to soften the hard, sheering effect of the tiny bike seat . . . so I added another pair, and then another. Yes, I donned three pairs of spandex shorts just to pad my ass enough to pedal through the day!

For the sake of ceremony, Toots rejoined me to cross the Rio Grande River into El Paso, a city she loved for its Tex-Mex food, artisan boots, cowboy hats, and turquoise jewelry. El Paso was also the last major airport for the next 750 miles that my sister Arielle could fly in to and that Toots could fly out from.

The Fourth

It was the Fourth of July and we were holed up in a dusty old RV park in Van Horn, Texas, just off Interstate 10, for a two-day rest stop.

My grandfather, Papa, happened to be hauling freight in his big-rig semitruck along the same route and stopped by for a quick visit. His big bear hug and endearing nibble of my ear made me feel five years old again. A nibble of my ear was his affection toward me for as long as I can remember, and it was also my offering each and every time I saw him. He drank a Coke, had a smoke, wished us all well, and took off down the road again, pulling gears.

Outside of town there was a small pop-up fireworks stand stocked with the good stuff—Black Cats, cherry bombs, Roman candles, screaming meemies, hoosker doos, hoosker don'ts, whisker biscuits, scooter sticks, and whistlin' kitty chasers. I didn't see a single snake or sparkler. We loaded up!

That night, on an old dirt road in the middle of nowhere, we lit the sky on fire with a symphony of gunpowder. A few locals lit theirs as well and made it a night to remember.

Ghost Towns

Southwest Texas was barren, windy, and eerily lonely. Once-thriving small towns now sat empty with old, abandoned relics of a time long since passed. We rode right down the narrow main street of a ghost town called Lobo. With its crumbling brick buildings, vacant motel, and empty shops, tumbleweeds literally blew across the street. The hair stood up on the back of my neck while I listened for the echoes of the cotton farmers and cowboys who'd once called this place home.

We stopped to rest just beyond the town's last structure, its faded roof collapsed like twigs. Our modern motor home sat adjacent to a dilapidated home that was at least one hundred years old. We sat there for a while, all of us in a deep state of contemplation.

"Damn big-box stores!" Bice blurted out.

Ben chimed in, "Yep, a cool little town like this is unfortunately the casualty of corporate America."

I added, "And here we are with this motor home stocked full of goods from Walmart . . . we're part of the problem!"

"No, dude, we would have shopped in this town if it still existed," Bice lamented. "Walmart just undercut the stores here and forced everyone to buy from them."

We hung our heads with a shared sense of loss.

For two weeks, we moved across what seemed like the true Old West. I imagined Billy the Kid and his compadres galloping their steeds alongside our bicycles, Texas Rangers in tow. I stared across the plain and imagined teepees encircling a fire as well as wild horses and covered wagons caravanning westward. My mind was wild with visions while we bucked a headwind into Brackettville.

Washed Sins

To our surprise, Fort Clark—a frontier fort founded in 1849 after the Mexican-American War and which was meant to guard the Mexican border and protect the military road to El Paso—happened to have a swimming pool! And not just any pool, but one of the largest natural spring-fed pools in Texas. The turn-of-the-century artificial pool was a three-hundred-foot, one-million-gallon oasis that stayed a cool sixty-eight degrees year-round and was fed by the Las Moras Springs (or "The Mulberries"). The spring waters were home for the Comanche and Apache Indian tribes that had inhabited the area in the sixteenth century. It was said that for eight thousand years these waters were the grounds for ancient life.

A sign read, "When you cross Las Moras Creek your sins are washed away."

But the feedwater creek was off limits to waders, and a walking bridge was the only legal access to the pool. Against everyone's warnings, I listened only to the omnipresent Indian spirit and slid down the mossy embankment into the water and crossed slowly . . . my sins sent afloat.

The Feud

We'd spent nearly a month in Texas; over eight hundred miles of headwinds and heat wore us down to a breaking point. Camped in a national park east of Houston on the border of Louisiana, I awoke to a commotion in the front of the bus. Tempers flared as bags were being packed. Hollyn, Zerbe, and Miles were adamant about leaving the tour and planned to fly out of the George Bush Intercontinental/ Houston Airport. I was livid and cursed the mutiny.

"What the hell are you guys doing?" I demanded. "Zerbe! Where are you going?"

"We're over this, Baker. We're going to fly out of here today!"

I knew I was to blame. For the past two months we'd suffered the agonizing monotony of cycling consecutive long, hard days, sleeping seven bodies together in a cramped motor home, and suffering midsummer weather across the middle of the United States; it was enough to test anyone's mettle.

Complicating the situation further, Zerbe had developed personal feelings for Hollyn, of which I suspected. She was the proverbial lamb in a lion's den. Gorgeous, loving, and fun to be with, she held her own amid an RV full of alpha males. I caused the rift by being jealous of Zerbe and Hollyn's affinity for one another and was selfish with my feelings for her. I'd made the mistake of wanting a romantic relationship in such circumstances, all the while delusional about her feelings for me. We were all fragile and volatile and had been pushed to the brink.

Zerbe and I fought like brothers outside the bus, yelling and screaming at each other.

Zerbe threw his water bottle against the bus and I pounded my fist on the picnic table, asking, "How could you do this? Why now?"

"It's not my fault or hers; our feelings just happened!"

"You know I love her," I wailed.

"Yeah, well, she doesn't love you that way."

A sobering dose of reality from Zerbe hit me like a ton of bricks. Bice intervened like a referee with his composed voice of reason.

"Fellas, what the hell?" Bice demanded. "This shit isn't worth it! We're more than halfway there. Just let it go."

Our feud slowly fizzled out in the forest that day, and we reconciled with a hug. We let it go. Zerbe and I agreed to stay the course and finish what we'd started . . . but my feelings for Hollyn had turned into resentment—sadly, we both knew that she couldn't stay.

And Miles had other things to do back home anyway, so his departure was inevitable.

I dropped them both off at the airport and returned my attention eastward.

With a renewed sense of friendship and optimism of the road, there was an inspired new intensity on the bike and for our journey into the Bayou.

Mud Dogs and Dirty Bugs

For some reason, the moment we crossed over the state line into Louisiana, Bice and I adopted a thick Southern accent grossly influenced by the movie *The Waterboy* and the Cajun football characters therein known as the Mud Dogs. We spoke in character among ourselves and in the video blogs we shared online. I even tried this with a group of locals at a gas station—they took interest but soon caught on to my act.

Our spirits were high as Ben and Bice flanked Zerbe and me over the bumpy lanes along the Bayou. We welcomed this lush part of the country, which was new to all of us and a reprieve from the Western deserts we'd suffered. We sang iconic tunes like "Song of the South" by the band Alabama and Lynyrd Skynyrd's "Free Bird," our selected theme song.

Wilted tree limbs covered in long green moss and cobwebs with spiders galore sagged low along the cracked road. Rusty mailboxes marked graveled driveways that led up to hidden wood shacks and small shanties near ponds of water and along rivers with high green banks. Old rail bridges crossed land that was lush with flora; dense and overrun vines entangled most structures.

My accent remained for a week or so, long enough to annoy the guys and bad enough to attract a stranger's stare. I gave it up once we hit Mississippi.

The Cuts

Long, narrow two-lane roads fissured towering timberlands like the rows of a vineyard. The roadways, known as "cuts" in the thick pine forest, were single clearings between logging claims. I'd had no idea Mississippi had such dense woodlands or even a logging industry.

We sliced our way down the smooth black road through hot afternoon showers and steamy evening skies. At the end of the day, I showered off with a water hose next to a gas pump in the parking lot of a fuel station; I was wet and sweaty or sweaty and wet . . . there was no difference, it didn't matter.

I found Southern hospitality to be a true cliché. I was taken aback by the genteel nature of folks throughout the area, their open arms for hugs and open hearts for charity. The food was a convivial art form of camaraderie and comfort, with simple ingredients prepared with love. I fell in love with the Deep South . . . a place of old tradition and simple ways, a place that seemed lost in time and happy that way.

Hobby Gator

We'd crossed Lake Pontchartrain back near New Orleans to meet a family friend of Ben's named Hobby, a real Cajun aristocrat with his white-pillared plantation home and fresh crawfish gumbo. He inspired the name of our new mascot, a severed alligator head that sat in the dashboard of the bus: Hobby Gator. The taxidermic trophy was evidence of my visit to a gator farm and the first time I'd ever tasted the prehistoric meat. Fried, it tasted like funky shrimp; it was tough like steak and chewy like octopus, an acquired taste.

Jellystone

It was now late August, and to celebrate Bice's birthday, we over-nighted at the Jellystone family waterpark east of Mobile. The Yogi Bear–themed park provided RV hookups, water, and power but seemed all but vacant with few visitors and the swirly-tubed waterslides shut off. Zerbe must have worked his charm, because he strutted out of the main office with a smirk and a thumbs-up as the water began to flow down the waterslide.

"Wooo!" I hollered as I slid backward down the slide while Ben belly flopped into the pond below.

"Yewww, I'm droppin'!" Bice yelled as he launched into the top of the tube.

For hours we played like little boys, splashing and sliding, with Zerbe catching me in the shallow end just after I'd splashed down from the slide.

Waterspout

The green gulf lands of Alabama gave way to the white sands and turquoise water of Pensacola Beach. We had reached Florida, and a jubilant giddiness overcame the boys and me. We stopped for a day of fun and rented golf carts to tour the town.

While we relaxed under the sun near the beach, an ominous funnel cloud appeared offshore on the horizon. The growing black cloud snaked across the water like a belly dancer to song, misting closer every minute.

Naively, we stayed and watched in awe as beachgoers hurried off the sand and into their cars to flee the impending natural disaster. As the winds picked up, so did we . . . although slowly, because most of us had never actually seen a tornado in person, much less a waterspout.

"Wow, look at that thing spin!" Zerbe marveled.

"Unreal!" Bice agreed.

"We should probably roll out of here, fellas," I warned. "I've seen a tornado in Oklahoma, and they're vicious!"

The threat, however, dissipated in our rearview mirror as we drove off in our carts, hungry and in search of a meal.

St. Augustine Sand

We awoke with excitement for our final ride day, thirty-two miles straight through the oldest city in the United States and right up to the edge of the Eastern Seaboard. Yet there was a somber undertone as the coffee brewed while we all sat around the living room of the motor home. I sat at the window side table and took a bite of my oatmeal and then one of an orange wedge.

"Man, I can't believe it's almost over," Ben uttered as he slurped his piping-hot cup of coffee, his feet propped up on the couch.

Adam followed, "We've pedaled over three thousand miles, fellas; we should be damn proud of ourselves."

I nodded and pressed play on my MP3 player. The song "To Live Is to Die" by a favorite boyhood band, Metallica, reverberated loudly and united us in rhythm.

"Let's do this!" I exclaimed as I dropped my dish in the sink and headed for the door.

With one last huddle and a few high fives, we saddled up and set off down the narrow country road on the outskirts of town. The low-hanging Spanish moss gave way as we pedaled up and over the first of the many turn-of-the-century bridges that spanned the winding waterways through town. My heart raced as I caught a glimpse of the snow-white sand at Castillo de San Marcos, the seventeenth-century Spanish stone fortress that sat across from St. Augustine Beach . . . our destination.

I looked over at Bice as he danced on his pedals, his face beaming brighter than I'd ever seen. I then glanced back at Ben; he, too, was smiling, riding upright with his hands high in the air.

I patted Zerbe on the back as we both continued to pedal. I leaned forward against him.

"I love you, brother," I said. "We did it. Thank you."

Zerbe steered the bike left and right through the narrow wooden sign poles, our wheels skidding to a stop in the deep white sand.

The humid ocean air filled our lungs as we cried out: "WE MADE IT!"

Bice and Ben dumped their bikes and ran over to lift me off the tandem and into the air.

We chanted, "Rise above! Rise above!"

Toots ran over and embraced me; she and her friend, Dave, had flown in the night before.

"You've done it, buddy!" Toots cried. "We've come a long way, haven't we?"

I was overjoyed, with few words to say. Zerbe grabbed my arm. Also locking arms with Bice, Ben, and Toots, we shuffled our way to the water.

We celebrated in the parking lot with a small group of friends and onlookers who'd shown up to support us. Bice handed me a bottle of champagne. "Let's toast!" he exclaimed. I shook it and popped the cork the same way I did all those years before at the national championships. I couldn't help but think about that time, the last time I'd sprayed it in celebration. Sea soaked and dripping with bubbly, I sat down to reflect on our effort for the camera . . . an impromptu interview of sorts.

Still buzzing from our feat, we spent the next few days relaxing and packing the guys for their flights home. On the final day in Florida, a warm storm blew in. I sat alone in the motor home all day, lulled by the rain while I awaited my dad's arrival. He was to accompany me on the long drive home, a swift four-day haul, straight through.

I remained in a state of euphoric reflection and marveled at the transformation that had occurred. I think Ben had the most dramatic change; he morphed himself from a cigarette-smoking (pack-a-day), stress-eating, film-industry man into a lean, mean cycling machine in just over three months. We were all impressed by his commitment. Bice and Zerbe had chiseled themselves down to hardened athletes, with tan lines and confidence in their eye. Everyone seemed to be completely satisfied in every way.

I myself felt a new level of ability both in my body and mind and felt like I could do anything. I was more motivated than ever for the next phase of my life—rehab, work, or whatever was to come.

Aimless

On the heels of the tour, I'd been home for only two months when my mind had become restless and depressed. Tired of the back seat, I didn't want to ride the tandem anymore. By the time we'd reached St. Augustine, Florida, I had pedaled thousands of miles behind the sweaty derriere of whoever was in front. It was time for a change . . . to progress to the next level. After all, that was the point all along . . . to use the bicycle built for two as a stepping-stone to one.

My issue was that I was strong, my body was primed for pedaling, and I felt ready to try to ride on my own, but I didn't know of a way to safely ride independently. I felt like I had plateaued without a way to progress. I was aimless with nothing to focus on; I felt defeated.

I sat in the garage and shared my frustration with Toots.

"I need to keep going!" I exclaimed. "There has to be a way for me to pedal on my own."

I then explained a vague idea I had of a three-wheeled bike and how maybe I could ride such a thing, but I was doubtful.

"If you can build a safe bike like that to ride on your own, we'll do it again," Toots said.

"Do what again?" I asked.

"The tour; we'll ride across the country again!"

That statement planted a tiny seed of possibility in the back of my mind, and Toots knew it. All I needed to do was water it.

I began to research my next step.

Independence

With my painfully slow dial-up internet connection, I discovered a small, passionate group of tricyclists in Europe. The old tricycling heritage was strong in Belgium and parts of the United Kingdom, but was nonexistent in the United States . . . except for Stu Flax.

Stu had cerebral palsy and at the time was the only known competitive tricyclist in the States. In the late 1990s, he'd built a custom tricycle to race in the International Paralympic Games. I learned that Stu also had an up-and-coming protégé named Alex Mask.

Alex, like Stu, had cerebral palsy and lived in Florida. The two of them trained together, raced together, and swapped custom parts for their specialized racing trikes. I studied their sport and learned their unique three-wheeled world and prepared to emulate what they were doing. I followed their journey through news articles, race results, grainy photos, and old videos. I dug deeper to uncover Alex's contact info and called him.

"Hi, Alex, my name is Aaron Baker; I just want to tell you, you are a rock star on three wheels, my man," I gushed, knowing that Alex was one of only two people in the entire country to race the machine I was enthralled by.

He was a legend in my mind, doing something I aspired to do, a similar inspiration like Pat Rummerfield. I couldn't help but lead into our conversation with praise.

He responded in dry yet quirky corporate phone etiquette, "How may I help you, Aaron?"

"I have followed you and Stu for a while now. I would love to ride a tricycle too! Who do you recommend I reach out to for a trike of my own?"

Alex was gracious with his time and answered my questions; he then passed along a personal contact: a man in the United Kingdom named Geoff Booker.

Geoff was known throughout Europe for his handcrafted tricycles and was just the man I was looking for, so I called him. Our spirited phone chat ended with Geoff tasked to build a custom conversion axle to be fitted onto my bicycle frame.

KHS Bicycles had been my tandem bike sponsor for the past few years and was excited to support my new cycling endeavor by providing one of their frames for the conversion. The combination of a Geoff Booker–built axle and a KHS carbon fiber frame was to be the first of its kind and only the third racing trike in the United States.

Alex called back randomly a week later. "Hey, Aaron! Did you contact Geoff?"

"I sure did. He is going to fabricate an axle for me. Thank you again!"

"You're welcome, but you'll need to train on a bike while Geoff builds the axle; it could take a couple months."

"I know, you're right. That's why I train on a spin bike in the gym."

"No, no, you need to pedal on roads. That's why I'm going to give you my first bike, the recumbent trike I learned with."

"WHAT! Alex, I . . ."

"Just pay for the shipping and the bike is yours."

"I don't know what to say, Alex. THANK YOU!"

"Just promise to pay it forward when you're through with it."

"Absolutely! WOW!"

Technically, as an unemployed dependent of the state and still recovering from my injury, I could not afford expensive equipment like the trike. It was only because of Toots's fiscal thriftiness, corporate sponsorship, and kind acts from people like Alex that I was lucky enough to receive such an opportunity.

A wood crate arrived a week later. Inside was a bright-red-and-yellow recumbent cycle, road worn and ready for me to ride. Alex was six feet tall and skinny like me, so no size modifications were necessary.

I sat down and reclined in the seat; I held the vertical steering controls on either side of my waist and clipped my feet into the pedals stretched in front of me. I grinned from ear to ear and pushed forward on the pedal; the cycle moved easily.

"All right, I'm rollin!" I hollered.

I'd spent years cycling on the tandem, but this feeling was new and liberating. I was moving the machine autonomously, completely under my own power. It felt like a go-kart . . . slung low to the ground, two wheels in the front and one wheel in the back; a stable yet nimble configuration. I was overjoyed and immediately set out onto the Paseo bike paths near our house.

Two months flew by as the recumbent consumed my attention. Training rides were independent and downright fun! It was my first real sense of riding a freedom machine again, hearkening me back to the same joyous feeling of the motorcycle. At my own volition, I'd speed up, slow down, swerve, and skid my way round. The proverbial gate was swung open and I was set loose.

Three Wheels

A brown rectangular box postmarked from the United Kingdom arrived at our doorstep. It was heavy, littered with tape, and had clearly been abused by its travel through the mail. I tore the packaging like it was Christmas morning. Geoff had meticulously wrapped and labeled every single piece of custom-made hardware. I felt honored to own a piece of his craftsmanship and couldn't wait to assemble it.

The next day I sat in the bike shop and watched Bob the mechanic assemble the pieces. At age twenty-seven, I marveled just like I had at three years old at the wheeled machine that would carry me far and fast. I stared at the newly assembled tricycle that was stirring to be ridden. My maiden voyage would be a huge leap into the unknown. I was nervous; I knew that a mistake would certainly lead to further injury. I had always been the passenger on the tandem, only responsible for my balance and power on the pedals. Now I had to not only push the pedals, but I also had to shift the gears, slow and stop with the brake lever, and steer for control while I held my entire torso up on a tiny seat! This scared me. I worried that my body wouldn't respond to my brain's commands. I had to convince myself that I could do it.

It was a cold, dreary day at our old stomping grounds at Lake Balboa, the site of my first ride. I sat on a black foldable stool set alongside the trike. I swiveled my left leg up and over the frame. I braced myself— with one hand on the seat and one hand on the stool—and carefully stood up. The bulbous plastic cleat on the bottom of my cycling shoes made me feel like I was standing on ice. I could barely keep my feet under me, let alone walk.

While straddling the bike frame, I held on to the bullhorn-shaped handlebars and squeezed the front brake lever with my dominant left hand. I leaned left to lift and finagle my right foot on to the clip-in pedal. With a firm click, my shoe locked onto the pedal. I counted down from three in my mind, similar to the start sequence on the tandem ... three ... two ... one. I stepped down onto the right pedal to lift and clear my butt over the seat. Once seated, I spun the crank to the twelve-o'clock position for my left-foot insertion. Snap! Both feet were locked onto the bike.

I sat motionless for a moment with my eyes closed and listened to my body; from my toes to my nose, I felt the tension in my muscles along with pressure and subtle pain. The bike seat, a tiny sliver of leather, was immediately uncomfortable. I opened my eyes and pushed hard against the pedal. I was off ... a new level of ability and independence commenced eight and a half years after my injury.

What a feeling it was! The crisp winter air kissed my cheeks as cold beads of water whisked up from the front wheel. My Lycra-covered legs turned the pedals, my muscle memory in full automation. As I picked up speed, the handlebars shimmied and quickly reminded me that this was dangerous. The trike forced me to think a lot! I had to think way ahead, preempt maneuvers, and premeditate my body movements to remain safe and in control.

With every turn of the pedals, though, my smile widened. Memories of cycle control flooded back to me, easing my adaptation to the physics of a tricycle.

A conventional tricycle—two wheels in the back and one in the front—is an awkward device. It has a high center of gravity and can easily tip over, especially when cornering. Also, because of the two wheels in the rear, a tricycle does not lean left or right to counter a road's camber. Instead, I had to counter lean off the opposite side of the seat and handlebars . . . a technique that was quite difficult for me. Furthermore, the gyroscopic effect of a spinning front wheel for balance does not apply to a tricycle. I could never sit up and let go of the handlebars to ride without hands. If I let go of the handlebars, the front wheel would just flop side to side and surely end in a crash.

The practice rides didn't last long; they were quickly replaced by hard effort and data. It was liberating to be independent, but it was difficult and risky to ride. It was not something I did for pleasure, especially without a goal. It actually angered me. I remember the thought on my third ride—I can do this! If it's this hard to ride one mile, then I'm doing it again . . . I'm going to ride across the country. My rationale being, I'm taking too much risk and working too damn hard for a leisurely, insignificant ride. I needed to transform the difficulty into a purpose greater than myself and an adventure worth exploring.

I declared it . . . only this time not to an audience, but to Toots—affirming the seed she'd planted three months before.

It was January and my goal was to continue the Rise Above Tour with a start date of June 10, 2008. I had a ton of planning and preparation to do, not to mention building my capacity and testing my skills on the trike. Six months is a very short window of time for this type of undertaking. My advantage this time was that the infrastructure was already there: the tour bus, sponsors, and logistical know-how. All I needed to do was declare the mission publicly to hold my feet to the fire and then go back to the beginning and set a short-term goal . . . like the LA Marathon.

The Fourth Time

Toots and I had already completed this iconic event three times—2003, 2004, and 2006—so I thought it was the perfect opportunity to announce the tour and test my abilities on the trike. The LA Marathon was scheduled for March 2, 2008.

The night before the event, I parked our sponsor-laden tour bus near the Los Angeles Coliseum adjacent to the start/finish line and stayed the night. We awoke at 4:00 a.m. to a gathering of familiar faces outside the bus, bustling with bicycles and coffee in hand.

This go-round we had an entourage, which had been organized the month before. Adam Bice and Ben Marius brought a slew of friends and supporters to ride with us. We also invited people I worked out with at the gym and alerted the local news. We had a spirited group of thirty-five riders and gave everyone matching black shirts with the new logo we wanted to debut.

Adam Bice was a graphic designer by profession and helped me design the C.O.R.E. (Center of Restorative Exercise) logo with our bright-orange Rise Above phoenix as the "O." We had it printed large across the front of the shirt, which made us stand out as a recognizable group. C.O.R.E. was the name of our dream rehab center; this center did not exist yet, but we promoted it like it did.

With the sun rising at our backs, our branded peloton pedaled along Exhibition Parkway parallel to the University of Southern California. I felt strong on the trike and proud to see our show of support. I upshifted gears to show Bice how much stronger I'd become since riding with him on the tandem.

"Yewwwww, Baker," Bice yelled. "Looking strong, bro!"

This was the first time anyone had seen a trike like this and was a cause for much inquiry. Interested folks casually rode up alongside me and asked questions about the trike . . . who made it, why I ride it, etc.

The innocent questions were nice, but I could barely breathe out a string of words to form a reply . . . let alone have a conversation while pedaling. It took everything I had to ride that trike. Every single pedal stroke required my maximum effort and 100 percent focus. There was no room for thought, just focused movement and pain management.

I'd chastised my fitness trainer once while I was struggling during an exercise. "If I had your body, I'd win championships," I said with a snarl.

It was a rude comment, I know, but I was in the heat of battle with my body, and he was belaboring on about his swollen knee. Soon after I apologized and acknowledged the truth—that pain and suffering are relative.

By mile seventeen my legs and lungs were screaming, my internal temperature was rising high despite it being sixty-five degrees of morning air, and my head was pounding. My inability to sweat turned my skin clammy, and I started to become dehydrated. These were the beginning signs of a dangerous domino effect toward autonomic dysreflexia.[1]

I was so hell-bent on finishing the 26.2 miles, double the distance I'd ever gone on the trike, that I dismissed these warning signs and pushed through with my head down and eyes up.

---

1 Autonomic dysreflexia (AD) is a potentially life-threatening medical emergency that affects people with spinal cord injuries. It indicates overactivity of the autonomic nervous system—the part of the system that controls things you don't have to think about such as heart rate, breathing, and digestion.

A noxious stimulus (which would be painful if one could sense it) below the injury level sends nerve impulses to the spinal cord; they travel upward until blocked at the level of injury.

Since these impulses cannot reach the brain, the body doesn't respond as it normally would. A reflex is activated that increases the activity in the sympathetic portion of the autonomic nervous system. This results in a narrowing of the blood vessels, which causes a rise in blood pressure.

Nerve receptors in the heart and blood vessels detect this rise in blood pressure and send a message to the brain. The brain then sends a message to the heart, causing the heartbeat to slow down and the blood vessels above the level of injury to dilate. However, since the brain is not able to send messages below the level of injury, blood pressure cannot be regulated. The body is confused and can't sort out the situation.

Our group had dispersed by mile twenty, leaving only Toots and Arielle alongside me on the tandem, with Adam Bice in tow. My recollection now is only of my pinhole vision and muffled hearing. I have seen photos of myself at the final turn and have been told stories of those last few miles. Honestly, I don't remember much because I passed out and collapsed off the trike when I rolled across the finish line. I was picked up and carried to the paramedics and nursed back to consciousness.

I remember waking up inside the tour bus later that morning and wondering, *Was it all a dream? Did I actually ride the LA Marathon?* I peeled back the blankets and found myself still wearing my urine- and bile-soaked riding gear.

"Yeah, I did."

I lay back down and closed my eyes with a grin.

The LA Marathon was a success; it was all I needed to prove to myself that I had what it took to ride across the country again.

I had three more months . . . plenty of time for the little seed that sat dormant in the back of my mind to germinate after that event. I had just added water. The clock was ticking, though; days were flying by and D-day, June 10, was coming up fast.

Besides my original cross-country route (the Southern Tier), there were only two other cycling-specific routes west to east across the country: The Northern Tier from Washington State to the coast of Maine (4,293 miles) and the Trans-America Trail from Oregon to Virginia (4,215 miles). I chose a modified version of the latter by adding the Western Express route (1,577 miles). In total, my planned route would take us from the Golden Gate Bridge in San Francisco, California, 4,202 miles right to the steps of the White House in Washington, DC—across the middle of America.

R.A.T. 2

A small crowd gathered around our Rise Above Tour bus, which was parked in a lot next to the sand just north of the Santa Monica Pier.

This was our dress rehearsal and send-off party for all our Southern California friends and sponsors.

Toots and I were a skeleton crew of two this time around. I didn't want to burden my friends with another "Hey, you wanna ride bikes across the country?" phone call. We did, of course, welcome family and the occasional volunteer to be our support driver along the way.

For show, we suited up and pedaled a few laps around the parking lot, snapping photos, filming video, giving interviews, and sharing lunch to celebrate the continuation of the tour and its official start in two days.

By midday, we were loaded up and driving north to Morgan Hill for an overnight pit stop at the headquarters of one of my longtime sponsors. Fox Racing had supported me since 1995, when I won my first motocross national championship. Talent recruiter and rider rep Todd Hicks continued to believe in me despite my career-ending injury. His gesture of support was an incredible confidence booster during the early years of recovery. Todd often sent emails of encouragement, followed by boxes of my favorite clothing, protective wear, and gloves.

In addition to Fox, I was aligned with a handful of other companies and nonprofit organizations, including NuStep, KHS Bicycles, Rock Racing, Utopia Optics, Vega Nutrition, DVS Shoes, the Challenged Athletes Foundation, Life Rolls On Foundation, Road 2 Recovery Foundation, Disaboom, and HealthSouth—who all pitched in to support our four-month tour. The budget being $25,000, we carefully managed our resources along the way.

I rounded the corner and slowly entered the gated Fox headquarters parking lot, the bus barely squeezing by the low-hanging limbs of a massive maple tree. To my surprise, Todd had already marked off ten parking spots right by the entrance to the building. I pulled in with a bellowing HONK HONNNK! And without delay, Todd stretched a long power extension cord and water hose from the building to hook up to the bus.

"This ain't my first rodeo, bro," Todd said. "We hooked James Stewart's rig up just like this a few weeks ago!"

Before the sun set, we toured the building and visited every department. Todd paraded me around as though I were still a motocross star. I received hugs, high fives, handshakes, headshakes, and whistles wishing me luck. Like a kid in a candy store, I beamed with excitement as I selected anything I wanted from the shelves in the warehouse. Todd and I packed the bus full of gear and then sat for a few hours, sharing stories of racing and rehab over a plate of pasta.

The Start

The sun rose on June 10 and my eyes slowly peeled open. The Fox parking lot quietly stirred with morning birds but was soon interrupted loudly by lawn mowers and leaf blowers. Before the first employee arrived, we were already headed northbound to San Francisco: a forty-five-minute drive without traffic.

The route up Highway 101 stirred memories of the first time I visited San Francisco; it had been a quick, early-morning jaunt from our home in Carmel with Toots and Arielle. I remembered the sight of the land as it gave way to the bay. From the suspended steel bridge, I saw the city skyscrapers rising like castle turrets above the low, thick fog. It looked like we had entered a magical island with an ocean moat on which boats passed under another surreal red bridge. From afar, the Golden Gate captured my imagination.

Toots ushered me and Arielle across a bustling street downtown just behind a dinging trolley and a hurried mob, the morning workforce. The smell of bagels, coffee, seawater, and sewage swirled through my turned-up nose. With my head tilted back and my eyes to the sky, I stared up at the endless steel, concrete, and glass. I was awestruck and overwhelmed.

"Smile," a photographer said as she snapped a Polaroid headshot.

At that time, the Federal Building in San Francisco was the only place to expedite our passports for our impending trip to Indonesia.

I gazed at the mesmerizing Golden Gate with the same innocence of that first visit while I maneuvered the bus through the choked Bay Area traffic and parked it just below the southern side of the bridge. Old friends from Carmel were already there, readying their bikes for the day's send-off ride through the city.

It was just after 9:00 a.m. Toots, Arielle, and I ate oatmeal and drank coffee at the dining table inside the bus. I waved at familiar faces through the window and signaled them to come inside. It wasn't much conversation, though . . . mostly just energetic hugs and high fives. I was mostly quiet and focused. Unlike the first cross-country tour, this time I knew what I was getting myself into and had to continuously convince myself that it was going to be OK.

There was a slight breeze that carried salty air with a scent of tar-smothered piers and popcorn . . . the familiar smell of the Old Fisherman's Wharf. With little ceremony, Toots and I set off and pedaled amid a small group of cyclists along a bike path just across from the infamous Alcatraz Island.

Our send-off ride wasn't very far, eight miles or so. We pedaled from bridge to bridge along the coast and through downtown, across cable car rails and among slow-going traffic and pedestrians. The endpoint and final gathering for lunch was at the iconic Ferry Terminal at the east end of town near the Bay Bridge.

The most poignant moment of the day was when I looked over at Toots as she pedaled her own bike next to me, the grand Golden Gate just behind us. A realization occurred and emotion overcame me. I slowed and allowed the others to ride up ahead.

I coasted for a moment while tears welled up and fell down my face. There I was on my own bike, pedaling next to Toots—not behind— in the same place we'd embarked from so many years before. I felt a perfect alignment with myself and the path of life I was on. The impossible bicycle journey that I had chosen was ahead of me, in front of my wheels, and was not unlike all the other adversity that I had not chosen in life.

I had come a long way and I recognized that. I owed so much of my recovery and success in life to Toots. Gratitude surged through me. All I could do was stomp on the pedals and speed past the group with a smile.

"Let's gooooo!" I hollered.

It felt apropos to end the day at the base of the Mahatma Gandhi statue on Pier 1 with our tour bus parked just beside his likeness. Gandhi, a great visionary and empathetic humanitarian, led the world by example. I sat alone on a bench at his feet and pondered his actions and my own life, a parallel powered by suffering. Again, gratitude filled me.

As the sun slowly sank into the horizon, the golden rays—the glow for which the Gate was named—enveloped the communal table on the pier. A warm, freshly made sourdough bread bowl filled with thick clam chowder, a Caesar salad, and a sparkling Shirley Temple soda were the perfect denouement.

As we packed our gear and loaded our bikes in preparation to leave, a family of nine encircled us.

A young boy noticed what I was wearing and said, "Fox! I love Fox! We ride bikes too!"

"That's awesome, bud," I replied. "Where to?"

The entire family, mostly adolescent kids, had been cycling the country for the past year, living on the road, and had just arrived in San Francisco. I was amazed by their adventurous lifestyle and shared my stories from the road, ones that only those who tour-cycle could appreciate.

They wore regular street clothes to ride, day in and day out, which to me seemed absurd.

How lucky I am to have sponsors that support me and give me products to perform with? I thought.

Then I remembered—I had a big box of extra Fox riding jerseys, shorts, and gloves that Todd had given me.

"Hold on a second, bud," I said to the little rider as I turned and slowly stepped into the bus.

With an armful of gear, I said, "Now you guys will be Team Fox! Wear this stuff during the day while riding; it will feel much better in the heat."

Their squeals made my day. The kids chose their favorites while their parents shook my hand and hugged Toots.

"It feels good to pay it forward," I said to Toots.

We all hugged with Gandhi looking down over our shoulders.

With that, we were off. Our tour bus pulled off the pier and down the road, heading east to the first RV-friendly campground of the trip.

False Start

The next day we pedaled toward Sacramento, where my dad lived in a suburb called Orangevale. We stayed at his house for a few days while we finished up some pretour maintenance on the motor home, tow vehicle, and tricycle.

The tour bus had taken a slight beating the summer before during our first Rise Above Tour, with seven people living on and off it for three and a half months. We replaced the stained white carpet with stone-colored linoleum tiles in the living room and kitchen; serviced the diesel engine, electrical generator, and plumbing; and added new sponsorship decals to the exterior siding.

The new tow vehicle was a 2008 Ford van that needed a special driveline disconnector in order to be towed behind the tour bus. We had to wait an extra day for this special part to be delivered and installed onto the van. This set the schedule back a couple of days and began to stress me out.

To relieve the tension, take my mind off things, and keep my body in motion, I decided to ride around the American River near Folsom Lake minutes from Dad's house. This community was full of outdoor enthusiasts, with kayakers and boaters floating down the river, fishers casting from the banks, and tons of hikers and bikers cruising the tree-lined paths. I made my way around the river and over to the local bicycle shop for a full tune-up of the trike—new tires, a new chain, and new handlebar grip tape for my long tour ahead.

The Film Crew

The maintenance was finally finished on the tour rig, and we were confident to set out on the road once again. Dad would be behind the wheel of the bus for the next week while we headed east up the mountain pass. Interstate 80 toward North Lake Tahoe wasn't part of our cycling route; however, the little town of Truckee was where we would meet my friend—filmmaker Mike Hughes and his crew.

Mike documented Toots and me riding side by side through some of the most scenic parts of the Sierra Nevada; he followed us for three days around the lake, through South Lake Tahoe, and down the long, fast descent along Highway 50 into Carson City. Those few days were fun—and slightly stressful because of the bus being converted into a makeshift editing bay with five men living among us with their cameras, computers, and gear bags crammed in every open crevice.

Mike made us feel like rock star athletes, a skill he'd honed as a storyteller for ESPN, FOX Sports, and others. He'd taken interest in our story after learning about our cross-country ride the year before and had vowed to memorialize our effort this time.

He and his crew drove alongside us, hanging off the side and out the back of the van with their cameras trying to get "the shot."

They captured some of my favorite photographs and videos of the entire tour. The photos of us pedaling among fields of bright wildflowers, thick wooded forests, and rocky, snowcapped mountains tell a thousand words.

Our final night together was in a heavily wooded campground around an open-pit fire. Mike pointed the camera straight at me and began asking personal questions about the accident. He did the same with Toots. What he captured was a moment of intimate reflection, undocumented until then.

I spoke about my difficulties with paralysis and depression and how I'd contemplated suicide, and Toots opened up about her personal trauma and struggles with alcoholism. The moment was raw and cathartic. We felt vulnerable and exposed, but also relieved. We both knew that our purpose was to share it all . . . the good, the bad, and the ugly. It was the only way to reconcile our pain.

The Loneliest Road in America

Carson City is the last urban outpost before five hundred miles of what is known as the "loneliest road in America"—Highway 50. This was where we said goodbye to Mike and his crew and stocked up on fuel, water, ice, and food for what would surely be a long and lonely stretch of road. Dad had to leave, too, so it was now only Toots, Arielle, her little dog Mickey, and I left to tackle the solitary stretch of asphalt.

It was the end of June, and we were in western Nevada. The average temperature during the day was one hundred degrees, with little to no shade or reprieve at night.

The narrow, unmarked black-tar roadway split the sweltering salt flats like a fault line. Waves of heat radiated off the asphalt, melting almost everything that sat in place too long. Arielle kept the bus rolling close behind because of this danger, and at times the bus was also the only object to block the sun during the day.

Highway 50 was a popular Pony Express and stagecoach route during the gold rush in the mid-nineteenth century. The now-paved trail was littered with the remnants of old rusted mining equipment and abandoned mine shafts. The few ghostly towns were mere shadows of the past, haunted by the absence of life. And when we happened upon the few remaining souls who called those places home, we felt an eerie sense of being unwanted outsiders . . . spiriting us to continue on.

I felt that the hills did indeed have eyes as I rode through some of the seventeen mountain passes throughout Nevada, the most mountainous state in America. I couldn't help but daydream while pedaling up the crest of a pass, imagining the past and how difficult those times must've been. I imagined toting all my belongings aboard a wooden covered wagon pulled by a horse under the unforgiving sun. And just when I thought that I couldn't go any farther that day, I looked down at my twenty-first-century carbon fiber bicycle (a modern horse) and fancy shoes, then glanced behind me at our beautiful tour bus with the promise of reprieve . . . a cold drink, a shower, and a comfy bed in which I'd rest. That inspired me to push a little harder and farther, thanking out loud those gritty souls who'd come before me.

"I don't know how you did it," I whispered to the wind. "How'd you survive this place, in this heat, during that time? Thank you, Aho."

I nodded and pedaled on.

On the tenth unforgiving day along Highway 50, tensions began to run high. My emotional pendulum swung as I pedaled with anger, unhappy and in pain. The saddle rash between my legs was rubbed raw and wasn't getting any better; it stung with every spin of the pedals. I was sunburned, on the verge of a heatstroke, and unleashed venomous outbursts at Toots for no apparent reason.

She finally had enough of my attitude and snapped, "Dammit, Aaron, that's it! I'm not doing this! You can figure it out on your own."

She rode off to separate from me and did not speak for the entire day over two eight-thousand-foot mountain passes and across a vast, barren salt basin. By the end of the day she was at her wit's end with me and vowed to pedal on without us and the bus.

As Arielle helped me load up my bike and gear into the bus, Toots didn't stop and pedaled off into the night. We watched as she disappeared into the distance.

"This isn't right!" I cursed to Arielle. "She can't ride out of here alone; she has no food, water, or money."

I started the bus in a hurry and sped to catch her. I crept the bus along behind her until she slowed.

I pulled alongside her and leaned out the window. "C'mon, Toots, I'm sorry. It's not worth it. You can't ride out here in the dark!"

She stopped, said nothing, and boarded.

With few words we acknowledged that being out in no-man's-land was a life-and-death situation, and the only way we'd survive was by sticking together . . . in the very same way we had done all those years before. We hugged, buried the hatchet, and stayed the course.

Pedalin' Pete

The bus was running on fumes, nearly out of water and food, and we were still one hundred miles from Utah. The temperature was a hellish 120 degrees. Our rides had to be broken up into thirty-minute stints.

While we were pulled over to take a break from the heat, a weathered old man on a squeaky rusted bike with bulging plastic bags filled with bottles and cans hanging from his handlebars passed us. Stunned by the sight of this Lone Ranger riding eastbound in the middle of nowhere, we quickly packed up the bikes and boarded the bus in pursuit of this puzzling person. We thought for sure that he could use a rest, some shade, food, and water, so we drove fast to catch up to him.

I blew the horn with a friendly honk, honk, honk, signaling for him to pull over. He seemed reluctant to stop, but did. We approached him with our arms full of ice-cold water, Gatorade, fruit, and supplements . . . too much for him to carry with him, but enough for him to pick and choose from.

I introduced myself and commended him on his effort on the road he'd traversed, as Toots and I knew firsthand how hot and difficult the ride was.

"Pete," the sun-leathered cyclist said. "My name's Pete."

"Holy smokes, Pete! Aren't you hot in those fleece pants and denim shirt?" I asked brazenly while offering him a Gatorade.

He politely declined with a shrug.

"May we fill your bottles?" Toots asked.

"Yes, thank you," Pete said softly.

"Where are you headed?" Arielle queried.

"I'm going to Indiana to visit my brothers-in-arms," he replied.

We learned that Pete was a seventy-two-year-old veteran who'd made the road his home and had been cycling back and forth across the country for years before we happened upon him that day. I recognized the grit in his grin and saw that he was a living ghost of a bygone era—a breed of men who'd persevered through the harshest of times. These conditions were no big deal to him.

"I don't know how you do it, Pete." I recalled the story I'd imagined just days before. Here's one of those old gritty souls in the flesh—a cycling pilgrim carrying all he owns on his back.

Despite my offers of Fox cycling clothes, water bottles, sunglasses, and food, Pete was adamant to carry on as he was. So we said our goodbyes and wished him well as he disappeared into the heat from which he came.

So strange, I thought.

Toots, Arielle, and I looked at each other, perplexed by this odd encounter . . . then, without hesitation, we hurried back inside to the air-conditioning. The remainder of the evening we rested, conscious of our comforts, and reminisced curiously about "Pedalin' Pete," his unexpected impact, and our roadside Chautauqua.

Pedalin' Pete has since become a metaphor in my mind. His Buddha-like presence amid a hellish realm (literally) was the personification of Zen. Without luxuries, his disposition was simple, happy, and content—he was a resilient and steadfast man, *committed* to his journey. And despite enduring relentless suffering, he exuded a gracious joy and a grateful heart. I think of Pete often and reference our chance encounter . . . his example I try to live by.

Salt Lake City Stop

Cedar City marked a major milestone for us—the end of a two-week push across no-man's-land, devoid of life and services. We welcomed a scheduled week of rest. At this point of the tour, our eastbound cycling route intersected Interstate 15, a major artery that runs north and south from Mexico to Canada. From here, we drove three and a half hours north to Salt Lake City to pick up two additional riders and give a presentation at a rehabilitation hospital.

We'd structured our tour in a way that allowed us to pedal only east; we'd only detour north or south by car or bus for appearances and presentations or the occasional airport pickup/drop-off of our support crew. I was adamant that we would not waste our time, energy, and money pedaling in any direction other than east.

We made a KOA campground outside the city our home base for the next few days while friends and family stopped in to visit. Auspiciously, our neighboring RV housed Lance Armstrong's mother Linda, a celebrity in her own right . . . especially since Lance was, at the time, being broadcast on our TV inside the bus, winning the 2008 Tour de France. She chatted with Toots and me and watched on as we serviced our bicycles and gear under the awning outside. She took interest in our tour and the message we were sharing, especially the mother-son relationship—a dynamic we could all relate to. We exchanged information and hoped to cross paths again.

Joining Friends

In early May, before the start of the tour, my friends Jordan and Brianna had expressed great interest in joining me at some point along the route. I welcomed their enthusiasm but warned them of the rigors of this type of tour cycling.

"This is no joke out here," I strongly exclaimed during a phone call with both of them before their flight into Salt Lake.

Confident, both Brianna and Jordan assured me that they had been training to ride the pace and distance we were covering and vowed to make it all the way to Washington, DC.

"I've got this, buddy," Jordan assured me. "I've been riding my stationary bike every day for the past few weeks. I'll make it, no prob!"

"That's great, J," I replied. "I just hope you can handle the mountains and the heat."

Brianna echoed much of the same, "I have been practicing on my hand cycle and feel really strong, Aaron. I'm excited to join you!"

"Fantastic, Brianna. I just want us to be safe. It's really hilly and extremely hot! We've got a long ways to go!"

But it's one thing to ride thirty to sixty miles in one day; it's a whole other realm to do it day after day in hellish conditions in very remote places. It was downright dangerous and I knew this; that was why I'd taken up a stern leadership role among us.

Our first two days together in Salt Lake City were fun and lighthearted, filled with an appearance at a rehabilitation institute, a visit to a TV station for an interview, and an organized community bike ride around the park downtown.

Our new team consisted of Toots, Arielle, Brianna, Jordan, and me on board the bus. Brianna was a paraplegic after a car accident. Jordan, newly injured via a motocross crash, was more like me and walked slowly with a cane. Two camera guys, Rex and Dane, joined us to shoot the next six hundred miles . . . which would take us from Cedar City, Utah, to Denver, Colorado, in the span of about two weeks.

The fun-loving, happy-go-lucky guy Brianna and Jordan knew as their friend Aaron disappeared the minute we headed south to Cedar City. The bus was packed with the seven of us, four of whom had no clue what they'd signed up for. I was nervous because we were about to venture into a beautiful yet remote part of the country with little to no resources for help, if needed. And I was certain that we would need them.

Just sixty miles from our starting point, I was driving the bus with the music turned high . . . and the right front tire of the bus blew out. I slowed the bus and, as luck would have it, the nearest exit just happened to have a truck stop with a gas station and tire shop. The shop was closed but was scheduled to open the next morning at 8:00 a.m. We parked the bus, rolled out the awning, and set up our table and chairs to camp right there in the parking lot of the gas station.

"We dodged a bullet," I said to the newbies. "Had this happened while in the middle of nowhere, we'd be screwed."

Again, I warned them of the struggles to come. I suppose I was trying to scare them a little and sharpen their minds for the challenge ahead, as I was scared from the seven hundred miles of gnarly road we'd already ridden.

Honestly, I was pleasantly surprised by those first few days of riding. Despite Brianna having a tip-over crash and Jordan swapping back and forth between my upright trike and the recumbent trike, we were having a lot of fun, and they were riding well. We pedaled through warm rain showers flanked by high walls of vivid orange and vibrant red sandstone in Bryce Canyon and Zion National Park. We rode easily while being filmed from the van with the camera operator standing on the roof or hanging off the side to get a panoramic shot.

This part of the country is some of the most stunningly beautiful and awe-inspiring land I have ever seen. To be immersed so deeply, one pedal stroke at a time, was a very special way to experience it. I think we were all motivated to ride a bit harder and farther than usual, which caught up to Jordan on day four.

Sprawled out on the grass of our campground, he moaned and groaned from the day's effort. Jordan was a talented, young, up-and-coming motocross star whose career was unfortunately cut short by an accident. He'd suffered a spinal cord injury like mine and was recovering well ... so well that he was pedaling alongside me under his own power only two years after his injury, compared to the nine years it had taken me.

We rode on for another week along quiet, picturesque roads in southern Utah, through the Canyonlands National Park, Moab, and Castle Valley—our route followed our cycling maps, south of our next transition point where Jordan, Brianna, and the camera guys were scheduled to fly home from Denver, Colorado.

Thirty or so miles before our stopping point for the day's ride, a wide expanse of land opened up as far as my eyes could see—we were atop a vast, floraless plateau.

The horizon began to grow dark with ominous clouds that bellowed far-off thunderclaps and lightning snaps, the kind that light the sky and bolt the ground. Toots and I slowed behind Brianna and Jordan as they pedaled on. We glanced at each other with wide eyes. "A storm's coming, Toots!" I shouted.

"It sure is, and we're pretty exposed out here—no cover from a lightning strike!" she warned.

Arielle and the bus were nowhere in sight—too far up ahead for us to risk racing on. Just then the wind blew round and the temperature dropped. I shuddered and looked back at Toots again. "Oh no!" I pointed up at a vortexed mass of clouds swirling near—lightning was no longer our only concern. "Tornado! Hurry, Toots! Let's ride up ahead to that cattle-crossing guard and hunker down in the bar ditch alongside the road."

My adrenaline pumped as we blasted past Brianna and Jordan, signaling them to follow. "Down here, guys!" I waved, pointing at the steel girder in the ditch—the only solid object we could conceivably cling on to.

"Why are we huddling down here in the grass like this?" Brianna asked—Jordan, too, was confused by our anxiety.

Toots pointed to the sky. "See that little twirly tail dropping from beneath those clouds?"

"That's the beginning of a tornado!" I barked out over Toots.

Brianna ducked her head in her hands and whimpered a bit while Jordan looked up and gawked at the impending doom.

"We'll hang tight right here until this blows over," Toots encouraged—the wind howled stronger, hot and then cold all around.

Ten minutes in that ditch seemed to last an hour as the fast-moving storm blew through, the darkest portion changing course and passing us by. Luckily for us the tail never dropped and no harm was done, accept for maybe the psychological trauma of a near miss.

We caught up to Arielle and the bus and regrouped—Toots and Brianna retiring for the day while Jordan and I, still amped by the drama, chose to ride on into semiclear skies. Not long into the second half of the day, the winds kicked up again, so much so we had to cycle over into a covered parking area to wait it out—again, the bus nowhere to be seen.

Forty-five minutes later, I flagged Arielle as she steered our beautiful refuge on wheels round the corner and into the parking lot. Immediately I noticed the damage. "What the heck happened!" I gasped. The sunshade awning that stored tightly rolled atop the roof now hung half cut and dangling beside the bus.

"You wouldn't believe it, Aaron! The winds blew so hard back there, it felt like the bus was going to blow over!" Still flustered, Arielle went on, "You should have seen us! Mom grabbed a steak knife from the kitchen and climbed up on the roof to cut the awning as it flapped wildly in the wind—I tried to hold it steady while Mom sawed at the canvas. We were animals!"

"But why did you have to cut it? It was brand new," I implored, not considering the perilousness of their situation.

"Buddy, a gust of wind just about toppled us over—it snapped the awning fastener and bashed it into the side of the bus—it nearly broke the windows!"

"Holy smokes! I'm so glad you guys are all right." Relieved, we hugged, then boarded, and I assumed driving duty.

It was now nightfall and the crew was exhausted. We were at the crossroads of the route, a left turn north toward Denver and the airport. In the final few hours before their flight we reminisced about our time together. "You guys rode great! Nice work." I nodded at both Jordan and Brianna.

"It was a lot harder than I expected," Brianna admitted, and Jordan followed with, "Yeah, what an adventure!"

"That's what it's about, J, the adventure! We all faced adversity but stayed committed and forged ahead. We overcame a lot and I'm proud of us."

Toots and I ushered them and all their luggage to the gate, Arielle included, and watched as they boarded the plane. "I'm pretty sure they'll remember this experience for the rest of their lives," Toots said.

"I sure hope so. I know I will," I replied, and turned away to walk slowly with my cane.

The Highest Paved Road

Our bus was empty again . . . just Toots, me, and a new addition: Dave. Dave, Toots's old high school friend turned boyfriend came aboard in Denver to drive the bus and support us. We weren't keen on rejoining the map where we'd left off, so we chose to backtrack a little and pedal up and over Trail Ridge Road—the highest continually paved road in the United States—for novelty's sake. From 12,201 feet above Larimer County in the Rocky Mountain National Park, between Estes Park and Grand Lake, Trail Ridge Road was the best way for us to see the great Continental Divide.

Although the air was thin and ice cold, it was a refreshing reprieve from the lowland heat. The road was smooth from freshly laid black-top and zigzagged its way above the tree line. There were no other bicyclists at that altitude, only bundled-up tourists in warm cars or a few walking at the scenic turnouts along the way.

Toots and I felt great! We huffed and puffed our way up the steep grade; our breath blew like two steam locomotives as we slowly pedaled to the top. We paused at the overlook to take in the panoramic view of a prehistoric, glaciered valley . . . a real breathtaker.

An elderly couple moseyed over and nicely asked, "What are y'all doing way up here on bicycles?"

"We're riding across the country for those who can't," Toots replied.

"Well, that's nice to hear, dear . . . but what do you mean?" the woman queried.

I rolled in a bit closer. "I broke my neck in an accident, and I'm cycling as a part of my recovery and sharing this journey with others like me. And riding a bike is a wonderful way to see the country. Isn't it just gorgeous up here?"

"That's wonderful," the lady said. "Good luck on the rest of your ride!"

The couple waved us on as we turned and began our descent.

The bicycles, especially my three-wheeler, attracted a few other onlookers. As much as we wanted to stay and chat, we had to keep moving; it was just too cold to stop for long. We snapped a few photos and continued back down the mountain.

Sturgis

The following day I spoke to a group of newly injured patients at a rehabilitation center in Loveland, Colorado. I met an injured motorcyclist named Mo, who told me about an annual motorcycle rally held in Sturgis, South Dakota . . . only a few hundred miles from where we were. He described the event and how it attracted thousands of enthusiasts from around the world each year.

"You'd love it, Aaron!" Mo promised. "The rolling Black Hills of South Dakota are beautiful and the rally itself is legendary . . . motorcycles everywhere!"

I got excited!

"Why not, Toots?" I asked in front of the audience. "Let's ride our bikes through Sturgis during the rally."

After all, it was about to kick off the following week.

"Why not?" she said with a grin.

So, once again, we'd declared our intentions publicly and had to follow through.

We drove north to Deadwood, South Dakota, and pedaled east into Sturgis.

What a sight we must have been—Toots and me pedaling our bicycles down Main Street amid thousands of hard-core, leather-clad Harley-Davidson riders. At the stoplight, I sat wheel to wheel with rumbling Harleys in my skintight Lycra cycling shorts and tanned, shaved legs.

If there was ever a time to feel like the odd man out, it was then. But I didn't.

Toots and I had skulls on our jerseys and a rider's attitude. I nodded, waved the peace sign, and followed rider etiquette. We received looks, head bobs, and shouts of intrigue and disdain . . . but mostly words and gestures of support.

"Hey, rider! That's a hell of a trike you got there."

"You need a motor in that thing!"

"Y'all are in the wrong place with those pedal bikes."

"Good ridin'!"

We stayed only one night before we cycled our way out of town and climbed the steep, windy road up to Mount Rushmore, the famous monument of our forefathers. The narrow, two-lane road was lined with hundreds of parked motorcycles and their riders, who hollered like cheerleaders as we slowly cranked our way past. In the shadow of presidents George Washington, Thomas Jefferson, Theodore Roosevelt, and Abraham Lincoln, Toots and I embraced and laughed at each other.

"We must be crazy!" I cheered while glancing over my shoulder back down the mountain.

"We're in the land of Crazy Horse, son; it's in our Indian blood," Toots reminded me, referencing her Cherokee grandfather.

Woodward

We rode through rolling plains of yellow, windswept grass as far as my eye could see with the spirit of Crazy Horse, the nineteenth-century Lakota war leader for the Oglala band of Indians. It was his massive, unfinished monument that had inspired our bravery to ride among droves of speeding Harleys, wild buffalo, big rigs, and relentless prairie winds.

Our wheels finally turned southeast toward Oklahoma and into a parade of family and friends welcoming us.

Toots's grandmother and my great-grandmother, Granny Anna Irwin, came from the heartland of Oklahoma and was the matriarch of a large Cherokee Indian and Norwegian-blooded family. My kinfolk are sprawled all across the panhandle and the Chickasaw Nation; most of them now live in a small farm town called Woodward.

As we pedaled into Woodward, we were met by my aunt Sonja and thirty or so cars and trucks that waved flags and honked horns while they escorted us through town to Granny's house. Stuck in the lawn behind the white picket fence were two red, white, and blue campaign signs that read: Vote for Bowdy Peach—my bull-riding cousin, the same age as me, had apparently hung up his spurs for a bid at local office. Up the four distressed wood steps three of my uncles sat on the porch, rocking back and forth in their chairs, chewing tobacco, and talking about the weather. I rode my three-wheeler right through the swing gate and up the cement walkway to the steps.

"Howdy, y'all!" I hollered.

"Well, hey there, California!" Uncle Chuck hollered back.

I had always been known as the California kid among all the cousins. Age-wise, I sat right in the middle of the boys—Te, Bowdy, and Joshua—who were all at Granny's that day.

Still sweaty with our cycling shorts and helmets on, Toots and I walked up the steps and into the house, my cane shaky from my fatigue.

We saw Granny lying in a single medical bed in the middle of the living room, her head propped up with pillows. Her silver hair draped her face and framed a beautiful side smile. Half of her face had been paralyzed by a recent stroke that had left her unable to speak.

The entire family gathered around her bedside as Toots and I leaned in for a kiss, her eyes cheering our arrival. Without words, I felt her love; she communicated clearly with a gaze. As I kissed her cheek, I remembered when I'd been in that bed, unable to move or speak. I empathized with her and my eyes welled up.

Granny was the most tenacious woman I'd ever known—tough as boot leather, keen as a fox, and as witty as a comic. She'd survived the Dust Bowl era and raised my grandmother, my mother, and the rest of our family in a time that I can't even fathom.

I bowed my head in her presence and held her hand. I felt her bless me with a strong squeeze—a kind of "you can do it" moment. I sensed her passing onto me her mettle—a virtue I will carry on and honor.

That was the last time I would see my great-grandmother.

Speaking from the Seat

Wheeling through the automatic double doors, down the long hall-way, and into the gymnasium, I pedaled up to a podium microphone.

"Check, check." I tested the volume.

The audience jumped as feedback screeched through the speakers.

"Hey, all, thanks for having me today," I continued.

Hands clapped and faces smiled at me on my trike, an unexpected sight. I never even unclipped myself from my pedals. I sat atop my bike seat and delivered the talk to a group of doctors and patients at a HealthSouth rehabilitation institute in Tulsa. I reached down and grabbed my water bottle from the cage on the frame to quench my thirst midsentence, my helmet still securely fastened.

I described my journey from my injury thus far and happily answered questions, both personal and medical.

"How long did it take for you to walk?"

"What type of exercises do you do?"

"Have you ever considered stem cell treatment?"

"Can you have sex?"

In that moment, I felt 100 percent aligned with the message I was sharing. I literally rode my story into their lives . . . my words voiced not in hindsight but rather in the clear and present moment. My actions spoke that day, possibly more to me than to the listeners. As the doors closed behind me and the road opened up again, I pedaled east into the rolling Ozark hills, happy that my thoughts, words, and actions were all aligned . . . perfectly.

Those Damn Ozarks

So far, we'd pedaled more than two thousand miles up and over the highest mountains, through the hottest deserts, and across the windiest plains—but nothing was as downright difficult as those damn Ozark hills. Gaining no greater than two hundred feet in elevation, the steep, unmarked asphalt road undulated endlessly through a dense canopy in the Mark Twain National Forest. The sweltering heat was stagnant and hung low, moist with mosquitoes and fireflies . . . both tasted the same and got stuck in my teeth and on my skin.

The bus stayed close, never out of sight. Dave, still aboard, and very helpful along the way, drove while new recruit Uncle Kenny, whom we'd picked up back in Edmond, Oklahoma, sat shotgun . . . ready to assist us when needed. He was definitely needed.

We stopped every thirty minutes or so for quick roadside showers from a detachable shower hose and nozzle at the rear of the bus. Kenny, with a limp cigarette pinched between his lips, hustled iced rags from the cooler over to Toots and me.

"Y'all need some orange wedges?" he'd always ask.

We'd sit just inches inside the white line that marked the shoulder of the road with our feet propped up and drenched rags draped over our heads.

We paid no mind to passing traffic, as the bright-orange phoenix on the bus seemed to illuminate our presence enough for safety's sake. Cars often slowed and sometimes stopped to ask us questions.

"You guys a church band?" one nice fella asked. "Y'all on tour?"

Apparently that neck of the woods in Missouri didn't see too many folks like us passing through.

"No, sir, we're just riding our bicycles across the country," I said.

"Why would y'all do that?"

It was an honest question.

"Well, because we can," I replied. "A lot of folks can't. We ride for them."

More often than not, an innocent inquiry developed quickly into an in-depth conversation about my injury, family, friends, community, and—most often—God. Our presence on the road through the Bible Belt of America was nine times out of ten thought to be a religious undertaking.

A quick stop in St. Louis was not enough of a break to recover from the four hundred miles of Ozark toil. We needed proper rest . . . four or five days off the bike.

The Drags

I have been a fan of drag racing motorsports ever since my dad's pseudo marriage into the San Paolos, an Italian racing family back in Salinas. One time Uncle Mario, the Sicilian patriarch, made me and the other kids hide in the long, dark race car trailer while he and the rest of the family crammed four to a bench inside the wide-cab dually truck as we passed through the entry gate at the Baylands Raceway Park.

I sat inside the cockpit of the long, skinny dragster, gripped the butterfly steering wheel, and pulled the levers; my legs were too short to reach the pedals. I hummed my lips to make motor sounds the same way I did with the motorcycle, while the other kids shushed me to stay quiet. In the dark, I was the driver. I imagined rocketing down the drag strip first to the finish line, then slowing to a stop with the ballooned parachutes.

My imagination ran wild while at the racetrack, fueled by fumes and the thunderous sounds of the fire-breathing nitromethane monsters. To this day, I am still the little guy in the cockpit with the dream that one day I will rip down the strip.

I knew that there was an upcoming race in Indianapolis, Indiana, only 250 miles away from St. Louis. I convinced Toots, Kenny, and Dave that the slight detour from our route would be a great place to rest from the bikes.

Josh Baltimore, a dear friend of mine, was raised in a prolific drag racing family and had connections throughout the industry. He knew my passion for the sport and pulled some strings as a gift. I drove our obscure bicycle tour bus through the front gate of the famous Lucas Oil Raceway alongside the legends of the sport for the historic "Big Go"—the most prestigious race of the year. We parked our rig on the infield of the half-mile oval track next to the drag strip, nose to tail with John Force Racing motor homes. I was buzzing! We were camping among the greats in the sport for the next four days.

The first day happened to be August 29, Toots's fifty-fourth birthday. To celebrate, we decided to ride our bikes fifty-four laps around our campground, the banked oval racetrack. We began at 8:00 p.m., well after the sweltering sun had set and the track temperature had cooled.

By lap twenty-two, we had a cheering squad . . . famous drag racers and their families looked on and hollered as we pedaled past their smoking barbecues.

One family in particular stood at the track wall until we finished. Jimmy Prock, notorious engine tuner and crew chief for the AAA funny car driven by Robert Hight, had gathered his wife, kids, parents, and grandparents over to the wall to watch us. They greeted Toots and me with high fives and friendly hugs, as though we were already friends. We sat outside of their motor homes until late that night, sharing barbecue and our stories from the road.

Jimmy set his drink down and asked, "You guys pedaled all the way from California?"

"Sure did!" I replied. "Right past the old Baylands Raceway on our way out of San Francisco!"

I knew he'd recognize the reference to a legendary drag racing strip on the West Coast.

"My uncle Mario owned and tuned the famed 'Spaghetti Bender' dragster, which I dreamed of piloting as a boy," I added.

"Oh man, I remember that car!" Jimmy exclaimed. "The San Paolos, right? A big Italian racing family."

"Yep, that's them! It was through Mario that I got bit by the drag racing bug." I laughed.

By the end of the night, we felt like old friends. The young boys,

Thomas, thirteen, and Austin, twelve, were already eager to indoctrinate me as a brother into their loving family.

The weekend was sensational! The boys and I careened around the sprawling raceway on a team golf cart and visited Jimmy and his crew in the pits while they tuned the race car. We sat VIP at the starting line before every race and basically had unrestricted access to anywhere we wanted to go. The energy was intensified by the fact that Jimmy's car had made it to the final round. We were all abuzz with excitement in anticipation for the race.

As the lights went green, the exhaust flames flew high and both cars thundered down the track. Three and a half seconds later, at a speed of 331 miles per hour, Jimmy's "Prock Rocket" race car won.

A dogpile ensued at the starting line, crew members piling one on top of the other in jubilation. Fireworks lit the sky, signaling the finale. What an extraordinary way to end the day . . . with the team, our new friends, as the champions of the year!

From the seat of my trike, I watched the awards ceremony and subsequent photo shoot.

"Come on over!" Jimmy whistled.

He waved Thomas, Austin, and me into the victory circle with the car and team. I pedaled in front of the race car and positioned my trike between Jimmy, car owner John Force, and driver Robert Hight. I could not believe what was happening. I was awestruck! I hadn't been on a winners' stage since before my injury, let alone one with my racing heroes! The light bulbs flashed, followed by hoots and hollers, high fives and hugs . . . another revelry.

On a high, we parted ways with the Procks and the drag races. It was time to focus on our racetrack . . . two long lanes of open road heading to Ohio.

A Dogged Encounter

We were hauling ass! With the wind at our back, Toots and I flew along flat farm roads and cornstalks as far as the eye could see. We typically rode between twelve and fifteen miles per hour, but we zoomed an average of twenty that day! It may have been because we were so well rested from our time off the bike, or maybe we were just jazzed by the recent race event, but either way it started as a glorious day.

We had just rejoined the road after a quick lunch stop when Dave and Kenny passed by in the bus. The plan was for them to drive ahead ten miles to our next rest stop and wait for our arrival. Again, the wind was in our favor and pushed us along at an accelerated pace.

"Yewwww, we're flyin', buddy!" Toots yelled from behind.

"Hell yeah we are, Toots!" I sang back.

At that speed the flat roads were fun, so we pushed harder to keep the pace and the intoxicating feeling. The road narrowed with closely flanked cornstalks that reduced the shoulder lane into a bar ditch. My heart raced because of the increased danger.

Now going twenty-five miles per hour, we passed a green, lumbering tractor that bogarted the road with its flatbed trailer. Toots was right on my rear wheel, I shifted up another gear and pushed even harder. Adrenaline surged and the pace went up even more.

I heard dogs barking in the distance as oncoming traffic approached in the other lane. Ahead on the left, I saw a white two-story house with a low picket fence and a large, sagging tree. My peripheral vision slowed enough to see four short-haired hounds gallop across the grassy yard and burst through the crooked gate and onto the road. The passing car narrowly missed the first dog as he leaped across the lane, determined to attack.

I swerved my wheel to dodge his bite, only to look back at Toots as she, too, attempted to evade him. Like a kamikaze, the red-haired hound careened into her front wheel, lifting it up into the air . . . instantly slamming her onto the rock-hard asphalt.

I skidded to a stop and screamed at the dogs, "HEYYY! Get out of here! Beat it, you little bastards! Scram!"

They dispersed back toward the house.

Toots tried to stand and remount her bike, but her arm was severely bloodied, and she couldn't hold the handlebars; her face was bleeding too. In a panic, I told her to lie down while I raced ahead to retrieve help from Dave and Kenny.

Eight hours, two screws, and five inches of metal wire later, Toots's elbow was reconstructed and fastened back onto her left arm. She'd sustained a massive blow to her arm and the left side of her body and remained in the intensive care unit for the next five days.

"I'm so sorry, Toots," I said. "I swerved to avoid that first dog and then tried to—"

She interrupted, "It's OK, son. There was nothing we could do. I'm just glad you didn't crash too!"

"Dammit, Toots! I hate seeing you in here like this. And the horrific memory of you hitting the pavement . . ."

"Those damn dogs!" she sneered.

The Role Reversal

With her arm heavily bandaged and held in a sling, Toots sat back on the pillows, Dave, the ever-vigilant steward, had stuffed behind her back as Kenny and I watched. She clipped her feet onto the pedals and grabbed the right handlebar with her good hand.

"Can you fasten my helmet, Kenny?" she asked.

My backup bike, the red-and-yellow recumbent cycle Alex Mask had sent me, had become the chariot that carried my injured Toots.

She was adamant about finishing the final four hundred miles to Washington, DC, however she had to. Her persistence was the grit I'd seen in my great-grandmother, the personification of an Indian spirit; it was also the gift Toots had given to me . . . again, another imbued example of commitment.

I had the honor of following her while we rode. I became the guardian, the support rider, the rock for her to rest on. Our roles had reversed in a magnificent way. We were allowed to experience a fuller spectrum in our relationship, a deeper empathy, and a clearer understanding of each other.

We pedaled over the Appalachian Mountains and through our country's history. We rode beside horse-drawn buggies across Quaker settlements and through old coal-mining towns lost to time. The limestone cutaways and long, looming tunnels opened up to the District of Columbia, our nation's capital and the epicenter of etched, white marble that entombs the echoes of our past.

On a cold, dreary September day, four months after we'd begun, Toots and I coasted along the Reflecting Pool at the Lincoln Memorial in Washington, DC . . . the end point of the tour. At the feet of Abraham Lincoln, I stared out across the mirrored water and then looked over at Toots. There were no words.

Racing Again

On a whim in 2006, before the Rise Above Tour, Toots and I drove to San Diego to visit the US Olympic Training Center in Chula Vista . . . the home base for our country's athletics program. From the back seat of a golf cart, we looked out across the sprawling campus while on a visitors' tour. We were there with the intention to find new inspiration for my continued recovery.

Fast-forward three years to 2009, and there I was, driving our Rise Above Tour bus through the guarded rear-entry gate with athlete credentials hanging around my neck.

My dear friend and mountain bike legend Tara Llanes and I were selected to attend a weeklong athlete discovery camp, where emerging athletes of different abilities can potentially be chosen to begin official Paralympic training in pursuit of national and international events for USA Cycling . . . the ultimate goal being the 2012 Paralympic Games in London.

"Woo-hoo!" Tara hollered from the passenger seat while leaning forward to get a better view out the side window. "We're here, dude!"

She pointed at the far side of the campus and added, "Oh, man, look! There's the new BMX track!"

"We're doing it, T!" I exclaimed. "We're actually going to train like Olympic athletes!"

I maneuvered the bus horizontally across five parking spaces in the paved upper parking lot west of the athlete dormitories, auditorium, and cafeteria. From the bus's living room window, I saw the Olympic rings left of the BMX course with an oval running track and emerald green inner field just below. I watched in disbelief as Olympic athletes in training pole-vaulted and high-jumped right in front of me.

As I shut the engine off, I thought about the visitors' tour and the dream I'd held since. Wow, here I was again . . . but this time as an actual athlete, prepping to train as an Olympic hopeful. It felt surreal.

"We're damn lucky to be here, T!" I rejoiced.

Athletes don't usually show up with accommodations like an RV; more often they take up residency in the dorm rooms on campus. But since I was fresh off my second cross-country bicycle tour, I was granted special clearance to park on-site.

I quickly learned that the US Olympic Training Center was under heavy surveillance and shrouded in secrecy. I equated it to being a cross between an open-air college campus and a full lockdown penitentiary. Our country's best athletes train in private, away from prying eyes and Peeping Toms. This was a world few people ever get to see, and I was awestruck at this opportunity. I knew I would have to ride harder and push myself further than ever before just to prove I was worthy of being there.

That first evening, after finalizing the check-in process—tons of paperwork, fingerprints for their files, and photos—we began with athlete introductions in the auditorium at the center of the campus. Twenty or so Paralympic hopefuls sat facing a stage bookended by bay windows that overlooked the training grounds.

Olympic staff and coaches were introduced one by one to explain their roles and the details of the coming week. Head Coach Craig

Griffin then went around the room for an athlete roll call, during which each of us had a few minutes to introduce ourselves and our background.

Slightly embarrassed, I admitted that I was the one with the big black motor home on the hill and apologized for taking up so many parking spaces. But I then quickly pivoted with an invite to all for after-hours PlayStation video games and Gatorade. A communal laugh made me feel welcomed and excited for the week.

"Eat something power packed," Coach Griffin yelled as we left. "Tomorrow's ride is going to be a doozy."

The cafeteria was just down the hall and around the corner, its hallowed walls lined with framed posters of Olympic legends like Michael Phelps, Jackie Joyner-Kersee, Carl Lewis, and Muhammad Ali. In the virtual presence of these icons, we also sat shoulder to shoulder with current Olympic stars; each round dining table had six people.

The buffet seemed relatively straightforward, other than the quality and quantity of the foods offered. Some meals were already predetermined for longtime resident athletes who had specific performance needs.

I chuckled inside as I scooped a dollop of mashed potatoes.

I can't believe I'm eating like an Olympian, I thought.

It was a small plate of mashed potatoes, grilled veggies, a lean chicken breast, and a bit of pasta, nothing special. The Olympic rings that branded the plate made me feel like I was consuming superfood, being fueled for a heroic effort.

Eight in the morning came fast, and the blacktop parking lot outside the bus door was abuzz with activity. All coaches, support personnel, and cyclists were geared up and ready to roll. I clicked into my pedals and sat on my trike amid the group while Coach Griffin briefed us on the day.

Otay Lakes Road was a very narrow, roughly paved stretch of country road with little to no shoulder for bicycles. This sketchy strip of asphalt was going to be the main route for most of our test rides.

The first training ride of the week was called "out and back." It was a placement test, with each new athlete being closely followed by a coach; each coach was a former professional cyclist or other type of athlete. The objective was to just GO as hard and as fast as possible down Otay Lakes Road to a designated turnaround point and then back. There were no instructions other than that.

Easy enough, I thought as I sat in a single-file line waiting for my turn. We were sent off in thirty-second intervals, with the people presumed to be the fastest (based on our individual disabilities)? I started third and quickly hit my maximum effort against the infamous Otay headwinds.

I was a seasoned cyclist at this point, having consistently ridden four to six days a week for the past six years . . . not to mention across the country twice. I was used to giving my maximum effort at different times during a ride. I quickly learned the major difference between tour cycling and racing—no rest. From the moment the stopwatch begins, the pain ensues. The pros call it the "pain cave." Those who can go deep into the mental "pain cave" and remain there the longest are usually the ones who win.

Competitive cycling is not at all a pleasant sport; in fact, it is a masochistic exercise of suffering.

What did the pain cave feel like?

Shit. Absolute shit.

First off, my legs went through phases of pain. They exploded with power down through the pedals and felt great, but only for a minute or two. Then they began to throb, burn, and spasm, shaking violently against the pedal rotation. I called it "pedaling squares."

Next, my muscles fought against smooth, circular motion. In training or on tour, all I had to do was let up, relax a moment to reduce the spasms, and then carry on with momentum. But when the clock is ticking and you're racing for medals, there's no letting up.

After about ten minutes of initial suffering, I'd hit my sweet spot, a narrow window of absolute performance. All my physiological systems were in sync; a steady heart rate, oxygen uptake, fluid circulation, muscle contractions, and exhalation were all rhythmic and harmonious . . . the zone.

Then my heart rate would spike . . . 160 to 180 beats per minute is fine for a short stint, but we're talking twenty to thirty minutes. I thought my chest would explode! I swore that my lungs bled; I tasted iron in my mouth when my body went past my anaerobic[2] threshold (the point during exercise when your body must switch from aerobic to anaerobic metabolism). Lactic acid filled my veins, and my blood pressure became erratic . . . high, then low, then high again, then . . . blackout.

These are all pretty common signs and symptoms of extreme physical effort, but these can be life-threatening for me.

The name of the game was management . . . to push to the very edge, stay there as long as possible, and not fall off.

Coach Rick Babington pedaled behind me without comment; he watched me struggle, suffer, and fade across the finish line. His only task was to observe my riding technique and identify areas of improvement. He came to me later that day after lunch with a list of suggestions.

"First of all, you're pedaling way too high of a gear with a slow, difficult pedal cadence," Rick said. "If you mash too hard on the pedal, you will fatigue sooner. Second, you're downshifting too late when approaching a hill; if you time your shifts better, you'll maintain your pedal cadence, workload, and momentum. Third . . ."

I stopped him.

"I understand the theory, but have you ever trained a recovering quadriplegic on a tricycle?"

"No," he responded.

"I'm not arguing with your suggestions; I just need you to know more about my body, my physical strengths, and weaknesses, because

---

2 Muscle pain, burning, and fatigue make anaerobic energy expenditure difficult to sustain for longer than a few minutes.

I've adopted these patterns out of necessity. I will literally fall off the seat if my legs spin too quickly. I use the slow, hard resistance as a balance tactic to stay upright against gravity, because my arms won't hold my body weight."

"Interesting," he replied. "We will have to work more on shift timing then and develop your cadence and body position over time."

"Sounds good, Coach. Thank you for understanding. My body wants to perform; we're just going to have to figure it out together."

As much as I wanted to be coached by the very best, I knew that no one knew my body better than me . . . and if I was going to improve as a cyclist, I would need a very special coach.

The end of five days of spirit-crushing rides, brutal road testing, classroom sessions, and group discussions came quickly. All that was left was the ominous final time trial.

The athletes talked about Honey Springs Road all week; it was a steep, unforgiving climb known as a proving ground for any Paralympic hopeful. This final uphill race against the clock would separate the field and narrow the coaches' final selections. I started fifth, thirty seconds behind the fourth-hand cycle.

I was toast within the first three hundred feet, exhausted from the week of work.

This is going to be ugly, I thought.

I knew I wasn't going to post a fast time. Every rider passed me, and I was now the slowest going up the hill. My only focus became . . . just finish it.

My cave was dark; with only seventy-five feet to go, I could barely see anything. Through pinhole vision I could make out a single figure standing beside the road at the top of the hill; the white support van with Olympic logos was behind him. Those rings were my target; I would die before I gave up.

Dry heaving, convulsing, spasming, and urinating on myself, I finished it, collapsed into the coaches' arms, and smirked. Rick smirked back.

"Great job, dude," Rick said. "You did it."

"I didn't make the cut, did I?" I asked, out of breath.

"You were slow, yes. But you gave it everything, and that means the most—it's our Olympic creed . . ."

> **"The important thing in life is not the triumph, but the fight; the essential thing is not to have won, but to have fought well."**
> —PIERRE DE COUBERTIN

In that instant, I could tell that Rick was my coach. His linebacker stature, baritone voice, and drill sergeant demeanor had intimidated me all week . . . but in that moment, he shifted into a deeply empathetic human being.

Rick and I became close friends beyond cycling. I came to learn and love his contrasting worlds—incredibly driven and structured, but also light, spiritual, and freethinking. He incorporated a variety of Eastern and Western wellness techniques like mindfulness meditation, massage, and a type of sound therapy called Acutonics into my training program. We made a great team and set some ambitious goals together.

Goals:

- USA Cycling National Championships, 2009–2012.
- World Cup Championships, 2009–2012.
- Paralympic Games London, 2012.

At this point, I had not entered a legitimate race in ten years. While the LA marathons and charity rides were challenging for me, they were leisurely at best. I needed to jump straight into the game and force myself to race. Rick constructed a timeline of local weekend races in which I'd participate, slowly building me up to compete at a premier annual event—and teaching me the value of this quote:

"You do not rise to the level of your goals. You fall
to the level of your training."
—Navy SEALs

My life was evolving again, quickly progressing from rehab riding to race cycling. Not unlike the early days of recovery, every single aspect of my life was analyzed and optimized for results. I ate, slept, and drank cycling. I took daily naps in a personal hyperbaric chamber just so that I could recover faster to ride more.

Two and a half years and a national championship later, Toots and I came to a crossroads. For many years, we'd dreamed about opening our own rehabilitation facility; we just never had the resources or credibility to do it. We were, however, at a point where our kitchen table plans might actually work. Do we continue the all-encompassing Paralympic pursuit or dump all our eggs into one basket and open our gym? We needed to make a decision . . . now or never.

TO MY YOUNGER SELF

We are all on a journey of a thousand miles. The quality of every single step counts as they add up to affect the quality of our life. Our daily choices matter, because they can become habits, and our habits evolve into behavior that ultimately defines our character—who we are and what we stand for. I look at the mirror on the wall as my ally, with the power to become who and what I want to be in life. My reflection knows all my secrets and shortcuts. It holds me accountable to my *commitments* and the choices I make. I do not look away. I own that power, the responsibility and the gift that it is, and I use it to fuel my next steps.

Scan the QR code and head to therebelliousrecovery.com/commitment for this part's complementary photo gallery.

Beginning

Awareness

Surrender

Inspiration

Commitment

PART 6 # Serve & Share

"We rise by lifting others."

Manifesting a Dream

The Center of Rehabilitative Exercise (C.O.R.E.—I later changed it to *Restorative* Exercise) was an acronym Toots, Taylor, and I came up with while sitting around our kitchen table sometime in 2003. Toots and I wanted a newly injured person to come through the door of our rehab facility and experience the same spark of inspiration and shift in perspective we'd felt at the Center of Achievement. We wanted that door to produce an overwhelming feeling of possibility, like a warm embrace or a hug of hope, to reassure a client that they were in the right place. Re-creating this feeling, this door effect, was our primary objective when designing the C.O.R.E. concept.

No single person—not a doctor, coach, or fitness trainer—could incite an energy shift as transformative as the vortex force of a sacred space—a place of community and connection. In essence, we wanted to connect people to themselves by connecting them to each other.

We truly believed that "if we build it, they will come."

Armed with only a small savings, Toots and I set out to find a space to rent. We scoured the San Fernando Valley of Los Angeles, planning to remain near California State University, Northridge, and the students, training staff, clients, and friends we knew. Our goal was to re-create the Center of Achievement outside of the state university system.

But many property management companies told us no. A single mother and her disabled son knocking at your door with a handwritten plan and penciled logo asking to rent the building was a risky bet. We didn't have a gym business background, assets, or any history of accountability . . . yet we kept knocking.

Our chapter-changing day came when we happened upon a recently closed Wells Fargo loan office. We peered through the dark windows and quickly noticed that the space wasn't on any brokerage lists.

My girlfriend at the time worked for another Wells Fargo branch and made a phone call to her manager. We got lucky when her connection allowed us to bypass a broker and get directly in touch with the property owner.

On paper, we didn't have a chance of qualifying for the lease; however, this time the property owner's family was friendly with one of Toots's dear friends and former business associates from her days as an importer. The friend gave a glowing character reference that boosted Toots's credibility.

With a signature, all our eggs were in this basket. Every single penny to our names was on the line and committed for the next five years when we signed the lease contract and accepted the key to our 1,700-square-foot future.

Toots, Coach Rick, and I sat in an empty room designated to be the office and had a coming-to-Jesus conversation.

"Honestly, can we open this business and continue to pursue the Paralympics at the same time?" was the question we asked each other.

We knew that building a new business and training for the Paralympics were each a full-time commitment. In my mind, though, there wasn't a choice between the two; we had to do both.

"This is a gym!" I exclaimed as I clipped onto my stationary spin bike—the first piece of exercise equipment we installed. "I can eat and sleep in this place."

"All I need is the fitness equipment and a futon in the office," I added as I pedaled.

We concluded that we were already in deep water, being committed to a lease and heavily invested in performance cycling. We had to stay the course . . . to build the business and continue the Paralympic pursuit.

The Dirty Work

Our first step before opening to the public was to renovate. We had to rip up the glued carpet squares worn out from a decade's worth of banking foot traffic. We thought it wouldn't be too big of a project once the carpet was removed—we'd clean the exposed concrete; place some rubber mats, logos, and equipment; and be finished with the flooring.

We were very wrong. Once the carpet was removed, thirty years of prior businesses conducted atop the floor were revealed. Multiple layers of glue, linoleum, and grout stood out like a tie-dye nightmare. The only options were to recarpet or grind the entire thing down to the original slab. That's fine if you have the budget and a large crew, but we were dealing with personal pennies and each one was allocated already.

I called my dad and asked if he would help us with the general improvements. This was exciting, because of my fond memories of joining him on his jobsites when I was a boy.

Dad agreed and drove the six hours down from Sacramento with a truck full of tools and cheerfully led the labor from there. I loved working with him; we had an unspoken communication, an uncanny understanding. I walked him through the empty space and shared the vision we had—the color of the walls, where the large mirrors would go, what each private room would become, and how we envisioned the floor.

"The floor is your biggest problem right now," he said with a chuckle. "It's hideous! I suggest we rent a floor grinder and get to work."

We were all on the same page, and with a little less than two months to opening day, we wasted no time and began grinding. I maneuvered the hand-pushed, circular grinding machine that was a lot like a lawn mower, just bigger and much heavier, while Toots followed on her hands and knees with the vacuum. This was a tedious labor of love, filthier than I could have ever imagined. For five days we literally faced the floor and the grueling task of stripping hard layers of solid concrete, a quarter inch every four minutes. It was brutal.

By the time the final coat of polish was dry, we were completely in love with our work; moreover, we were proud that we did it ourselves. I sat in the corner of the room and admired the floor. It seemed symbolic—a metaphor of our past and now, literally, the foundation of our future work and the solid base for someone like me to take their first steps upon.

Every inch of our gym was meticulously thought out. I imagined having a curved welcome countertop desk just inside the front door instead of a prefabricated piece of furniture.

"Like this, eh?" Dad asked. "What if we did it like that?"

"How about matching the curve of the countertop to the curvature of the ceiling soffit?" I replied.

"Perfect! Then the whole thing would match the floor tiles too!"

This was how Dad and I bantered with each other as we drew the template on the floor.

He knew what I meant when I said we wanted a client to have the "door effect"—to be drawn in with curved aesthetics, warm colors, and strong industrial design. I wanted the look to be a combination of a high-performance race car shop and a booming record store, the absolute antithesis of the sterile hallways in a hospital rehabilitation unit.

Everything was surreal up to this point; we were going through the motions of construction and getting permits, but we never actually had the feeling of "This is real" until our sign was mounted and lit on the exterior wall of the building.

Toots sat next to me on the curb in the empty parking lot around 9:00 p.m. on a Friday night. I sat tall in my wheelchair, with my eyes wide and looking at the side of the dark building . . . three . . . two . . . one. Our phoenix sign illuminated the night sky for the first time! Tears welled in my eyes. Toots and I looked at each other in amazement.

"We've actually done it, son," she announced proudly.

"I am lost for words, Toots," I said, my mouth agape.

We stared at the glowing building, the moon backlighting the scene. Just then, a shooting star arced across the sky.

"We are doing exactly what we are supposed to do, son."

"I know, Toots. I know . . . together we rise!"

We hugged and continued to marvel at the wondrous sight.

The next day, we proudly went to Gold's Gym, where Taylor

worked with his clients, and handed him a key to the front door of C.O.R.E.—the key to our future work together that we sealed with a handshake and a hug, our agreement, our pact.

Toots and I spent New Year's Eve cleaning and organizing the final details, as we were slated to open at 8:00 a.m. on January 1, 2011, paying no mind to the fact that it was a federal holiday.

On 1/1/11, we opened the Center of Restorative Exercise, a dream we'd manifested over the course of eight years from absolutely nothing.

I sat at the front counter, and Toots was in the office with the music playing loudly; there was no one besides us in the place. We hadn't hired any staff yet, and Taylor had yet to arrive. It didn't bother us; Toots and I were still high on the fact that our gym was open.

We paraded family and friends around anytime they stopped by. From 8:00 a.m. to 8:00 p.m. we kept our doors open, engaging any and all interested passersby. Those first few months of business were painfully slow; only a few community members and former clients of Taylor's signed up for memberships. And when the bills were due each month, we'd remind ourselves of all the people who were underserved and needed a place to go. *That's OK*, we thought and remained steadfast. After all, we were living the need.

Sometimes I'd joke with a new or potential client: "It's like the HairClub for Men commercial, 'I'm not only the HairClub president, but I'm also a client.'"

We printed brochures and flyers and hand carried them into every single hospital, rehab center, chiropractic office, massage parlor, and fitness facility within a thirty-mile radius. We were grassroots and passionate—it was our mission, our purpose, our life.

All In

It was sixteen months until the 2012 Olympic Games in London, and I had my work cut out for me. Rick had increased my ride schedule—one hard sprint workout or hill climb in the morning, with a longer-capacity ride in the afternoon, or vice versa. This was to be done two to three times a week, with moderate recovery rides in between. Recovery rides, for me, were never recovery, just more work. This type of effort warranted every fitness-training trick in the book just to help me sustain the load.

I napped in the hyperbaric chamber, which we kept discreet in the kitchen / break room of C.O.R.E. We had to keep the chamber private, because we didn't have the medical certification for others to use it. This capsule was a game changer for my productivity and gave me the energy I needed to work in the business and ride.

All the work was paying off; I was the fastest I'd ever been on a bicycle. My legs had grown in size and shape. I had to cut the inner seam of my underwear just to fit my thighs. My body had morphed into a cyclist's physique—skinny, farmer-tanned arms on a ghost-white torso and smoothly shaved, muscular legs with sharp tan lines midthigh.

I was a machine. I had spent more than a year focused solely on squeezing every ounce of performance out of my body. The tens of thousands of miles I'd ridden all boiled down to the few minutes on the stopwatch. On paper, compared to my international competitors, I was a shoo-in to win a medal at the World Cup. Rick was pleased with how I had progressed over time.

Toots, however, was concerned; she recognized the slow degeneration of my ability to walk. Instead of my cane, I was using my wheelchair more and more to conserve my energy between rides. I knew that I was sacrificing general function in everyday life for more performance on the bike. I had become a very proficient cyclist, powerful in my very specific way.

Without the trike beneath me, I'd become a wobbly mess. I had forgone my cross-training therapy sessions for more time on the saddle.

In the few remaining months before the games, and against Toots's pleas, I was making a conscious choice to grind myself into the ground. I was hurting myself and I knew it. Every training ride and mock race was an explosive expression of pain. I was channeling the fury of my injury into the pedals. I wanted to see how far I could push it, and I wasn't leaving a single stone unturned. If I didn't win, it wasn't going to be because of a lack of effort.

Backfire

What's the cliché? Work smarter, not harder. I learned this lesson the hard way. My body began to break down; my system was overloaded. While sitting at the desk in our office at the end of one workday at C.O.R.E., my abdomen suddenly began to tighten. A dull, throbbing pain quickly progressed to a sharp, stabbing sensation. Keeled over and leaning against the table, I couldn't move. Although it was painful, I played it off; I figured it might just be gas or bowel impaction. I said nothing while Toots finished closing up the gym.

"Are you ready to go?" she asked.

"Yeah, except I've got a little problem."

Wincing and still leaning on the desk, I added, "I can't really move from this position."

"How long have you been like that?" she asked.

"Oh, about thirty minutes," I replied half-jokingly.

"Seriously, son, don't play around. Can you sit up?"

The muscles around my entire abdomen were completely clenched, locking me in position.

"Ugh," I groaned.

The color was leaving my face, and my words turned into moans.

"OK, we're not messing around here," Toots said with alarm.

She quickly scooped her arm under my chest, leaned me into my wheelchair, braced me, and wheeled me out the door.

In a blur of pain and nausea, I lay in an emergency room bed, staring at my freshly painted, colorful toes and exposed, shaved legs. *Am I dreaming?* I thought to myself. I was two days away from boarding a plane to Rome, Italy, for the World Cup cycling event— Team USA and Coach Rick were already there. *This can't be happening.*

Rome was the final race before the games and the last opportunity to be selected for the Olympic team. I was lying in a hospital bed with an unknown condition, gradually getting worse.

Iodine was pumped into my veins to prepare me for a CAT scan. My eyes immediately swelled shut, followed by my throat. Clawing at my neck, I pleaded to the nurse that I couldn't breathe. I was having an allergic reaction. The terrifying memory of suffocation was all too real again.

I woke up, dazed and confused by the events that had unfolded. Through swollen slits, I saw Toots at my bedside.

"I guess we're not going to Rome," I lamented.

"Rome is the least of your worries, son. Your bladder nearly ruptured."

"Will you snap a photo, please?"

"Why would you want a picture of this?"

"I have to send it to Coach and explain why I won't be at the race."

With the press of a button, I ended my Olympic dream.

As Mike Tyson famously said, "**Everyone has a plan, until you're punched in the face.**"

I felt numb. It was a strange contrast between sorrow and solace. It felt like relief, to be honest; I guess because I knew that it was final. I had pushed and pushed for so many years to find my absolute limit physically and mentally, and this was it.

180°

I was sipping a mai tai in the cabana, poolside at the MGM Grand Hotel and Casino in Las Vegas.

"Damn, it's hot today," Brian howled, as he cracked open a cold Red Bull.

"One hundred and twelve!" I yelled back as the club music blasted in the background.

Las Vegas and the uninhibited debauchery of the town that never sleeps was the furthest I could get from my years of straight-and-narrow cycling life. I had done a complete one-eighty; I hadn't touched the bike in weeks and now sat bloated amid the party.

I was in a mental fog, an athlete's equivalent of postpartum depression. I felt aimless, drifting around without a goal in mind. I had spent twelve years working toward specific targets—learning to feed myself and walk again, riding across the country, and chasing the Olympics. *Now what do I do?* I pondered while floating in the convivial cesspool. *Forget it,* I thought. *I don't need to do a damn thing right now. I'm going to have fun with my friends and say YES to good times!* After all, Brian had plenty of adapted toys to play with. His Ferrari on hand controls, four-wheel ATVs, go-karts, a speedboat, fireworks, and more were surefire ways to help distract me from my woes.

Devine Timing

There weren't any parking spaces available close to the wedding ceremony I was attending; the wedding music was already playing.

"Damn, I'm late!" I said to myself as I circled the venue.

I pulled up close behind a catering truck and parked my imposing black, windowless van alongside a low rock wall. Perfect! The dirt lot was only feet from the grassy courtyard near the front of the little red barn where Jason, an old motorcycle-racing buddy, and his girlfriend Kristi stood facing each other. Their vows were mumbles as I walked carefully with my cane to the only open seat at the back.

"I do" was all I heard just after I sat down.

Everyone then stood up, whistling and applauding the newlyweds.

Better late than never, I thought as the DJ turned up and the dance floor filled with bridesmaids.

I leaned in and hugged Kristi, then fist-bumped Jason.

"Congratulations, guys!" I said. "This is a beautiful reception."

I leaned in farther and whispered to Kristi, "Are there any single ladies here you suggest I meet?"

Kristi smiled, winked, and pointed to the dance floor.

A pulsing amoeba of dresses and hair grooved to the beats from the booming speakers. Cocooned at the center of this mass was a brunette beauty with a cadence and rhythm surpassing all the others. She moved like an animal—a tiger to be exact—to the sound. I felt like Tony Montana in the infamous movie *Scarface*, when he first noticed Elvira.

"I like her the first time I laid eyes on her, I think—she's a tiger; she belongs to me," I quoted (to the best of my memory), snickering to myself as I watched from afar.

To catch this tigress, I waited patiently for her to tire and exit the dance floor before making my move. Just as I stood to take my first step toward an icebreaking conversation, she fell into the arms of another guy. Clearly she had a date. A boyfriend? A husband maybe? Of course she did! She was a knockout with a poise and grace I had never seen before. I thought this before ever speaking a single word with her.

The party eventually ended, and I left disappointed that I didn't at least get her name . . . boyfriend or not.

The moment I got home I became an internet sleuth, searching Kristi's Facebook page for friends or connections. I didn't have to search far, because Katelyn Devine was Kristi's good friend and a wedding planner. There were tons of cute photos of their girl gang.

"Yes, I found her!" I smiled to myself.

I clicked through to her profile. Her relationship status was "single." No way!

Sweet, I've got a chance, I thought.

I composed a friendly message and hit send.

Four days later, Katie, Kristi, Jason, and I were at a Mexican restaurant on a double date . . . our first date.

"Whoa, wait a minute, babe, I'll help you, hold on!" I beckoned from around the side of my van. There she stood at the back, in stilettos and a sultry black dress, bear-hugging my sixty-pound scooter.

"I've got it, I've got it!" she assured as she lowered it slowly to the ground, the deep squat revealing her smooth, shapely legs.

"Dang! You're strong—and sexy. I'm a lucky guy!" I said, winking and smirking as I sat, cane in hand, onto the scooter.

"Yeah, yeah." She blushed and turned to hold my hand as we made our way into the Ronald Reagan Presidential Library—the venue for the night's event—another hot date!

My injury and the accompanying complications and accommodations didn't seem to bother Katie one bit. In fact, she never really saw me as injured, as she'd later tell me over a meal. The more time we spent together the more she'd amaze me with her grace and generosity and capacity for love. She saw right through my adversity and loved me for who I was, not for what I was. I was so taken aback by her that I began thinking in a way I'd never thought before: *Is she the one? I'd be silly not to marry this girl. You'd better propose before she wises up!* It had been only eight months, but a flurry of nervous thoughts raced through my mind and my belly, spurring me on to plan the perfect proposal. *What kind of ring? Where should I do it? Who should be there? Uhhhggg!* I was an anxiety-ridden basket case for the few weeks leading up to the day. "Honey, would you mind wearing that pretty blue dress tonight, you know, the one I like so much?" I asked, hoping to seem nonchalant in my request.

"Why, what's going on? Where are we going?" she fired back, suspicious of my query.

"Oh, no big deal, I just really like seeing you in it, that's all." I turned to hide my poor poker face.

My plan was to have Katie come to C.O.R.E. after she got off work, around five, to meet me for a weeknight dinner date. Lo and behold, I had prearranged to have both her parents and sister present as I popped the big question.

Everybody on-site was in on it and hid behind pieces of exercise equipment as she sauntered her way across the parking lot toward the door. "Shhhh, here she comes, here she comes!" I hushed the excitement, and my stomach fluttered with butterflies.

Just then the song "Beautiful Day" by the band U2 began playing loudly over the speakers—she entered through the door. I stood in the center of the room with ring in hand, right between the large, fiery phoenix wings emblazoned on the floor—symbolic of my life up to that moment.

"Wait, wait! What's going on?" Her coyness gave way to confusion and then adrenaline as her beloveds emerged from hiding. She walked toward me, and I extended my hand and the ring. "Within these hallowed walls and upon this hallowed ground . . ." I went on to profess my love and proposed. With a squeal and flushed face, she said yes! We embraced, kissed, and celebrated with our families and friends all around.

Coming to My Senses

"Into the forest I go, to lose my mind and find my soul."
—John Muir

Katie and I had been together for a little over a year. We were newly engaged and finding our groove as a couple. I hadn't touched the bicycle for eight months and wasn't training for anything specific, just mostly enjoying Katie and the spontaneity of our relationship.

Most of my time was spent at C.O.R.E., where Toots and I focused on growing the business. My mind wandered, though. I longed for another adventure, another athletic goal to reach for. With both Katie and C.O.R.E. feeling securely established, I needed to refocus on my body.

Since I had created dysfunction by cycling as much as I did, I needed to reverse the holding patterns of bike riding. I had to focus on walking again, and I wanted to walk somewhere far . . . really far.

Two cars stopped and patiently waited for me to clear the crosswalk into the grocery store. I shuffled along behind the grocery cart, Katie picking and choosing her way around the market. Besides my blood pressure being a bit low from standing while waiting in the produce section, I felt rather confident holding on to the loaded cart with both hands . . . pushing it slowly, one tedious step at a time—a definite improvement upon my *walking on hands* analogy.

This is really good therapy, much better than the treadmill, I thought.

"Babe, doesn't this shopping cart help me walk better?" I queried.

"Watch . . ."

I lunged down the bread aisle, left foot, then right.

"Whoa, I've never seen you take such big steps like that before," Katie cheered.

"I know, right? I need to do more of this, like a lot more."

Where can I go to walk with a shopping cart without stopping? I thought. *A running track? The bike paths I'd ridden hundreds of times before? A quiet country road? Where could I buy a shopping cart?* My imagination swirled in the checkout line while Katie bagged the groceries.

Both of my hands held the outer edge of the steel push bar on the cart as the automatic doors slid apart, opening toward the crosswalk. A strong gust of wind blew at my chest as I stepped out the door; without that cart, I would have certainly sailed to the ground.

Just then, a vision appeared in my mind—a rock. Not just any rock, but the awe-inspiring "sailing stones" of Death Valley. The lone stone atop a vast, barren landscape that seems to slide across the hard, dry surface . . . leaving a skid trail in its wake.

Like a snail! I move at a snail's pace, I thought. A snail is in no rush . . . he carries all he needs with him and just cruises along.

I imagined myself in the desert like a sailing stone, walking with a cart toward the sun at a snail's pace.

My vision became clearer in the days following my epiphany in the supermarket parking lot. I began searching eBay and Craigslist for a shopping cart to buy, only to discover something better—a baby jogging stroller! A used jogging stroller made perfect sense; it had ample room for all my supplies and camping gear. It had three large wheels, plush suspension, and a front brake! Heck, this thing was made by the premier mountain bike company Giant Bicycles. I knew it would work!

I bought the stroller for $100 and began modifying it. I cut the seat belts and padding out of the main carriage and wrapped the handlebars with sticky cycling grip tape. I replaced the smooth road tires with heavy-duty knobby tires and added new brake pads. The biggest modification was to the front of the buggy—I used an electric saw to cut off the plastic foot plate to make room for a Rubbermaid office trash can to be fastened to the frame with zip ties and duct tape. The trash can was meant to be an extension of the carriage; it would carry my sleeping bag, cot, and umbrella.

The baby sunshade worked perfectly for my folding solar panel, which I affixed just in front of my two water bottle holders on the handlebars. "I've got to have electricity to charge my GPS and phone," I reasoned.

My life support cart, so to speak, was coming together. Like a snail's shell, I was taking my home with me. Everything I needed was going to fit inside this Frankenstein chariot.

Supplies:

- Folding chair
- Sleeping bag
- Sleeping cot
- Inflatable mattress
- Step stool
- Tool bag and tape
- Tire pump
- Solar panel
- Cell phone and mount
- Headlamp
- Umbrella
- Sunblock
- Portable toilet
- Urinal
- Nalgene bottle
- Thin doormat
- Garbage bag
- Coffee mug
- Hunting knife
- Small towel
- CamelBak water pouch
- Hiking backpack
- Two water bottles
- Handlebar light
- Goggles
- Sunglasses

- Hiking boots
- Athletic shoes
- Compression socks
- Two shorts
- Two shirts
- Two socks
- Two pairs of underwear
- Two gloves
- Windbreaker
- Down jacket

- Thermal underwear
- Hat
- Bandanna
- Three bungee cords
- Miscellaneous straps and ties
- Cane
- Five magic bullets
- Zip food pouch

Food & Water:

- Five gallons of water
- Twenty-five pouches of flavored electrolyte powder
- One box of instant coffee
- Fifty pemmican balls
- Twenty-five Hammer Nutrition bars
- Twenty-five energy gels
- Twelve dehydrated meals

Don't Go Alone

There was no way I was going to enter an adventure of this magnitude on my own, let alone in Death Valley. I had to have someone with me, and not just your average Joe. This was going to be a special kind of suffering, a discomfort unlike anything I had known before or could imagine. The painfully slow pace at which I was going to walk, the unrelenting desert sun, and the unforgiving remoteness of one of the lowest, driest, and hottest places on the planet was a downright dangerous proposition for almost everyone I knew.

I didn't want to ask Toots to put her body through another long adventure. At that point in our relationship, Katie had never done an expedition with me. So my next thought was my new friend Dominic, an Englishman and adventure athlete who also happened to be a journeyman filmmaker.

Dom had recently produced a six-minute short film called *All That I Am* that captured my Paralympic cycling bid. He sought to tell a broader story about my life history, recovery, and family, and he liked my plans to walk across the desert. He proposed to follow my journey with a camera and support me, if needed.

The point was to allow me to be as independent as possible but also be prepared with safety measures.

With only a few days left and all my plans in place, it was time for a dress rehearsal. I convinced Katie to join me for an overnight test session in a semiremote, high-desert campground an hour north of our house in the Santa Clarita Valley.

I needed to make sure that I could actually push the fully loaded, one-hundred-pound buggy across natural terrain. I had only practiced walking in my boots on the gym treadmill. Loose soil, deep sand, rocks, and brush were another story. I also needed to test my ability to unload my gear, set up camp, and sleep on my cot.

The test was going well until midnight, when the winds kicked up. I realized that my inflatable sleeping mat was extremely slippery under my down sleeping bag. Every time I changed position, I nearly slid off the cot. Between my sketchy sleeping arrangement and the howling winds, Katie and I decided to pack up, abort the test, and drive home.

The Weaver

"I am, therefore I do. Explore, I am the weaver. I
do, therefore become, a seer, and believer."
—MAYNARD JAMES KEENAN

I turned the volume dial up on the stereo to overpower the loud hum of the treaded tires against the highway while I listened to Maynard sing. My windowless cargo van was crammed with my fully loaded desert buggy and Dom's pull wagon, which we nicknamed "The Pig," to haul his camera gear and supplies, my wheelchair, and more. Toots sat passenger, while Dom straddled the Pig in the back.

I didn't say much during the two-and-a-half-hour drive northeast to our drop-off point. I played and replayed the song "The Weaver" by Puscifer. The lyrics became my internal mantra and set the tone for what I was about to endure. I was entranced.

Toots fidgeted in the seat next to me, obviously nervous. She chatted with Dom over the music and posed rhetorical questions like, "I wonder what it's going to be like for you guys out there?"

I, for the most part, tuned out and kept driving. The song ended, and I snapped out of my trance just in time as I steered off the solitary two-lane road in what was essentially the middle of nowhere.

"Here we are!" I informed them. "I recognize that signpost and rocky landmark; it's the reference point I mapped out as our starting line."

I lowered myself out of the van, my boots touching the desert floor for the first time. It felt good; I felt grounded. My thoughts were calm while we unloaded the gear from the van. I sat down in my wheelchair and asked Toots to help me apply the first heavy coat of 100 SPF sunblock, a procedure we'd done hundreds of times before when we were cycling.

Dom pointed his camera at Toots and me, asking us questions for context.

"I assume you guys have done this before?" he asked, referring to the sunblock routine.

Toots said with a chuckle, "Nah, not that much."

Implying my sentiment toward her as she smeared the white paste on my face, I said, "Yes, we've done this a few times, Dom."

Again, his voice and motions became muffled and blurred.

I stared blankly at the mountainous horizon and sang "The Weaver" in my mind.

Those lyrics were magic; they were word alchemy that empowered me to weave my own destiny. I am not what had happened to me; rather, I am what I choose to become.

I hugged and kissed Toots and said:

**"The journey of a thousand miles begins
with a single step."**
—Lao Tzu

I'm not sure how long Toots stood there and watched me walk into the distance, as I turned around only once to wave about ten minutes after taking my first step. Step after step I pushed against the buggy's handlebars, slowly steering clear of tufts of brush and small volcanic rock.

If you were to look down from an airplane, this portion of the route was thickly grown desert bush—a flood runoff where a deluge had dispersed in the past, leaving remnants of sand and stone, tree limbs, and undergrowth. Straight and forward for the next mile was the only direction I was going.

That mile was all I could muster before the light faded, so I stopped at the edge of the wash to set up camp. This was going to be my first big test. Did I save enough energy to unpack the buggy's contents? I needed to do it in a specific order to actually achieve on my own without Dom's help.

I began by unfolding my foldable chair to sit down and unfurl the umbrella. While seated, I slowly assembled my sleeping cot. To inflate the sleeping mat, I blew like hell for ten minutes. Then I unrolled the foot mat, unfolded my sleeping bag, took off my boots, and unpacked the food.

Done! I sat back in my chair, exhaled with a long sigh, and marveled at the vastness of Death Valley. The air was hot and devoid of sound. I closed my eyes and breathed in a long, deep breath. Exhale. I did this a few times until . . . my phone rang.

173

The single bar of cellular reception was enough to signal a call from my uncle Kenny.

"AA [the nickname I'd been given as a toddler], what are you doin'?" Kenny, also known as Radio, asked in the trucker tone in which we often spoke.

"What do you think I'm doin'? I'm walking, man. I'm following the sun."

I was slightly irritated that I'd left my obnoxious ringer on. It had completely interrupted the serenity of the moment. I love my uncle, though, and so we chatted for a few minutes and then hung up.

"Over and out," I said.

That night I slept like a baby, lulled to sleep by the eighty-eight shooting stars I counted just before dozing off.

Day 2

"How'd you sleep?" Dom asked, waking me with his camera lens inches from my face.

My sleeping bag still pulled tight over my head, I laughed and struggled with the zipper.

"I slept so good. I saw some sweet shooting stars."

He continued filming as I finagled my way out of the bag and sat up.

The sun had just risen, and the heat was soon upon us. The unobstructed light was so intense that I had to wear my racing goggles to shield my eyes from rays while I finished my instant oatmeal. After breakfast I systematically repacked the buggy in reverse order, folding chair last, and set off.

For the first half of the second day, I was filled with optimism. I walked confidently across the cracked desert basin, smiling to myself and feeling full of energy. Two hours later, I needed to take a break. It was wicked hot, and this was going to be another test to see how quickly I could go through my checklist before passing out from heat exhaustion. I needed to establish a walk/rest routine to manage my time, energy, and risk: walk for an hour, maybe two, and then stop and repeat the above. From sunrise to sundown, every day.

Every hour, rest or not, I ate one golf ball–size restorative energy ball. The handmade superfood snack was formulated by teacher and health food specialist Jan Babington, PhD. Jan was Coach Rick Babington's wife and often fed his athletes during training camps. When I approached Jan with my plan to walk across the desert, she knew I would need a very special fuel to keep me going. One that would provide ample protein, carbohydrates, and micronutrients, yet would not spoil in the excessive heat.

"Pemmican! Have you ever heard of pemmican before?" Jan asked excitedly.

I shook my head no.

"It's what the American Indians would eat—dehydrated beef or buffalo, finely ground and mixed together with dried berries, molasses, and tallow."

"Hmm, sounds interesting. What is tallow?"

"Tallow is a rendered form of beef or mutton fat and is primarily made up of triglycerides. It is solid at room temperature and can be stored for extended periods without the need for refrigeration."

"Whoa. OK, I love beef jerky and berries, and sweet stuff, but won't tallow taste pretty funky?" I joked.

"Yeah, it's an acquired taste," she said with a laugh. "How about I mix up a few batches with different ingredients, and we'll see which one you like best?"

A week later, Jan lined up ten different containers on her dining room table.

"After making the first batch according to the original Indian recipe, I knew I had to tweak the flavor profiles," she said with a giggle and a wink.

"Well, I knew you were going to experiment a little . . . but dang, Jan. Ten samples?"

"Here, start with the original and you'll see what I mean," she explained as she handed me a marble-size bite of the more than two-hundred-year-old recipe.

"Eww, man, it tastes so gamy!" I mumbled while chewing. "Definitely an acquired taste."

"Yeah, that one is pure buffalo, blueberries, and tallow."

"No molasses?"

"Nope, Indians didn't always have access to molasses; this recipe is as original as it gets," Jan explained.

"OK, well, I will definitely need to try one with some sweet sauce in it."

I sampled the rest and found that I enjoyed one of the others. The ingredients I chose were fifty-fifty beef/buffalo mixed with dehydrated goji berries, blueberries, bee pollen, spirulina powder, honey, and beef tallow . . . total superfood!

Jan's nutrition plan for me was:

- Eat oatmeal for breakfast.
- Eat one to two balls an hour while walking.
- Drink one to two 20 oz. bottles of water and one 20 oz. bottle of electrolytes every eight hours.
- Eat a rehydrated meal for dinner.

I can honestly tell you that the pemmican balls were, by far, the best source of food fuel I've ever had. I experienced a ton of energy from a single ball and felt great between bites.

After my rest, I repacked the buggy and resumed my march.

"Left, right, left, right," I called out to my legs, instructing them to move.

I offered Dom an unsolicited reflection: "I'm not wearing any bracing! I used to have to wear a brace on every joint of my body just to stand upright." I then explained to him my "walking on hands" analogy.

Dom encouraged my memory while he ducked behind the berm of a water wash we were following.

"This is a great shot, man; keep going," he hollered.

I couldn't see where he'd gone from my position; apparently, he was capturing a good angle with his lens. I kept walking and talking—to myself, it seemed—while Dom darted all around me like a desert jackrabbit, camera in hand.

I kept my front wheel pointed southwest, in the direction I had gazed out upon the day before, the sun setting just off my right shoulder.

"I'm smoked," I said. "We should set up camp here, Dom; I have to do my program tonight."

"Program?" he asked, puzzled.

"Ya, my BP . . . bowel program. You know, Number two . . . pooping?"

Dom laughed.

"BP is what the nurses call it in the hospital," I explained. "A bowel program is the bane of existence for someone with a spinal cord injury. My life revolves around this schedule, and God forbid I have an accident."

I candidly shared with Dom that a bowel program (pooping) is complicated and time consuming . . . and definitely not intended to be done in the middle of a desert on a three-legged port-o-potty.

Again, Dom pointed his camera at me while I sat with a sliver of the sun at my back, the sky stained a mosaic of color.

Without shame, we sat adjacent from each other and continued to chat about the day, the route, and the mountain pass we were heading toward.

"I wonder how steep that ridge is up ahead?" I queried Dom.

"Our camp tomorrow night should be at the base of it; we'll know by then," he offered.

I clenched and looked directly into the camera.

"Duuude!" Dom cried.

"Well, that's what you get when you film someone indisposed."

I laughed and resumed pooping.

Day 3

Nature's freeway narrowed as the desert basin faded behind us, the terrain steepening with every step. I had been staring at what seemed to be a potentially impassable mountain pass up ahead. But as I continued my course, periodically looking back from where I came, I realized I was gaining altitude from the desert floor . . . lessening the imposition in my mind.

But everything hurt! My body was revolting; each step felt like I was wearing concrete boots and stepping on hot coals. My back, neck, arms, and legs began to tighten and spasm all at once, and I convulsed with every step. This was the farthest and longest I had ever walked before.

I stumbled on a stone and stopped for a moment atop a mound. I took a deep breath and surveyed my best line choice. I saw that the terrain was intensifying. There was no way around a sketchy descent into a sandy ravine.

I took another sip of hot water from my bottle, grabbed the front brake, and stepped forward down the hill. The crushed volcanic rock gave way under my boots. I squeezed the front brake harder, the brake squealing under the pressure. I leaned back to counterbalance the buggy as the front wheel skidded against the gravel.

"Oh no!" I hollered.

I leaned forward onto the handlebars, forcing the front wheel to wheelie up toward the sky. I tumbled down against the buggy and onto the ground. I was met by hot sand. Dom rushed over with his camera.

"Are you OK, man?" he asked. "What happened?"

"I'm good; I just wheelied out."

I rolled onto my back in the sand and sighed with relief . . . I didn't hurt anything.

I lay there for a while and realized that the honeymoon phase was over. The romantic thrill of the adventure was long gone, and now it was getting real and serious.

The fact was that if I got into real trouble, Dom would have his hands full trying to get me out of the middle of nowhere. The buggy's purpose, other than carrying my life support supplies, was actual life support. Our unspoken plan B was to discard all my gear, load me into the baby carriage, and wheel me out of there, if needed.

This scenario was beginning to percolate in my mind as I stared into the cloudless blue sky, just as a passenger plane flew across my view.

"I'll have a Mr. T's Bloody Mary mix on the rocks please," I said, pretending to place my order with the stewardess thirty thousand feet above me.

"Doesn't that drink sound amazing right now?" I hollered.

I lay there on the desert floor and flashed back to the memory of the day I broke my neck. The moment was familiar and frightening. My body was exhausted, heavy, and unresponsive. I knew that if I didn't get myself up off the ground, I would remain there indefinitely.

A boiling over of energy sat me up in the sand, and Dom helped me set the buggy upright. To get myself up against gravity is often futile without some type of device or someone's help. However, I'd come prepared.

A ten-inch step stool hung from a hook under my handlebars and was just within reach. I unfolded it and balanced myself against the hillside. I heaved my lower body up and onto the step.

"That's the first step!" I celebrated.

I placed my feet directly beneath my butt with my left hand on the corner of the stool and my right wedged onto the handlebar of the buggy. I rocked back and forth.

One . . . two . . . threeeeeeuhhhhhgggggrrrrrrr!

I summoned every ounce of energy, forced it down through my legs, and pushed off the ground.

I stood defiant against gravity and yelled, "Yewwwwww!"

I pumped my fist and said out loud, "Thank you, body."

In the distance I saw a clearing, a plateau at the edge of a canyon just below the crest of the mountain pass. This was my destination, our camp for the night, and the halfway point with a view.

With a final heave of the handlebars, I stopped the buggy just feet from the edge of the cliff, about one hundred feet above the ravine. I turned around to see how far I'd come. The pebble-strewn plateau overlooked the great Death Valley basin I'd labored through. The vastness expanded my perspective beyond the front wheel of the buggy for the first time.

"Oh man!" I shouted, presumably to myself, as Dom was nowhere in sight. "What a view!"

I quickly unfolded my camping chair and sat facing the openness, soaking in the warm valley breeze. The golden light of the sun setting slowly beyond the western edge kissed my face as I squinted, my mind melding into the moment.

The silence broke when Dom appeared from out of nowhere and asked, "Hey, mate! You fancy an interview?"

Exhausted, yet feeling a state of serenity, I nodded.

"What are you thinking about right now?" Dom questioned as I sat back in my chair, my feet propped and crossed on the buggy's wheel.

"I'm thinking about my friend Josh. He died not long ago from a spinal cord injury. He was so young."

Dom pressed for more.

"I remember the smell of his house. He was decaying from abscessed pressure wounds all over his body. He was neglected and just lay there paralyzed—a conscious corpse—dying. It really fractured me, Dom." I went on: "I watched him suffer the same injury I live with—with all of the secondary complications that make it so horrific and so challenging—he just didn't have the love, support, and care I've been so fortunate to have. That could've been me."

"How do you handle the mental aspect of your recovery?"

"It's very difficult, Dom. I've spent many years struggling psychosocially because everything is so damn hard for me to do, physically. It can actually become more paralyzing mentally than the injury itself."

"Do dark thoughts still enter your mind?"

"Absolutely. It's like system overload; I can't deal with it sometimes.

Doubt, fear, and rage creep in and I think, 'Shit, I could easily be pre-scribed medication for this or self-medicate. I could drink a bottle of booze and numb myself.' But it doesn't help me. It actually hinders me more and makes things worse. THIS helps me!"

I pointed at the horizon, referring to my self-imposed suffering of the strenuous yet soul-filling walkabout I was on.

"This is more therapeutic than anything I could ingest or take," I remarked.

I stared off and reflected further: "Seeing Josh die rocked me. From that moment forward I've started to ensure that the things I spend my time and energy on have some purpose, have some meaning, have something larger than myself."

The wind whispered softly as the cloudless sky spewed shades of blue, purple, and gold. I sank deeper into my chair.

Day 4

"Feet, don't fail me now!" I instructed my body. "Let's go! Errrrrrrahhhh!"

I had to dig deep into the all-too-familiar pain cave on day four, as I awoke that morning to spasms and a pinching lower back. I sat up on the cot, still in my sleeping bag; my abdomen tightened so much that it nearly took my breath away. My back muscles were now pinching on the nerves. I could barely get dressed and tie my shoes and needed help from Dom to load my gear into the buggy.

"This is going to be a long day," I said.

"Yeah, it's the most difficult portion of the route," he pointed out, gesturing with his finger toward the crest line.

Standing facing the upward slope was intimidating. I took short, shallow breaths, careful not to trigger a spasm. My back was incredibly unstable. I was unsure if I could take ten steps, let alone traverse the summit to the other side as we had planned.

I had only two options: abort my mission and be wheeled in the buggy out and around the backside of the pass . . . or carefully walk myself into flexibility and relief.

I chose the latter. However, once I got to a certain point, there was no turning back, and it was a dangerous place to get help.

Luckily the steep uphill portion, six hundred feet from camp, was not off-camber and was relatively smooth. The fact that I had to lean way forward to push the buggy actually helped stabilize my back. My theory worked; by the time the hill began to slant to the right and required more strength, my body was warm and much more stable.

To counterbalance the buggy against the steep slope, I hung the heavy sleeping cot, food bag, and water jugs off the left side to keep the buggy from rolling over. Even so, the buggy and I teetered to the right with every step . . . threatening to topple into the ravine five hundred feet below.

Dom kept a hand on the left side of the handlebars to help me negotiate a shallow yet sheer and rocky crevasse. This short crossing was by far the most technical and dangerous jaunt in the route. One misstep or falling rock and I, or the buggy, would landslide down the hill.

Ten tenuous minutes passed as I heaved and hoed my way, inches at a time, to the other side. Finally, after what seemed like an hour, I stood safely on ground flat enough for a rest.

"All right!" I hollered, pumping my fist again. "Damn, that was sketchy! This is no place for a recovering quadriplegic."

The ravine crossing was only the halfway point for the day; another quarter mile of off-camber descent and a rock-strewn foothill lay ahead. From this high-up vantage point, I also saw what awaited me on the other side of the mountain pass.

I gazed in astonishment at a perfectly flat expanse of desert—a dry lake bed as far as my eyes could see. It seemed otherworldly, like the moon or maybe Mars. The postcard view filled me with wonder and stimulated me with a needed boost of energy to propel me to its edge on this fourth night of camping.

I collapsed onto the cot; my boots were the first thing to be removed. I lay at the edge of desert oblivion, heat waves radiating all around me as the sun began to set. I stared at my candy-color toenails, wiggled them, and thought: *We've come a long way, feet. Thank you for carrying me.* Dom built a fire and we both melded into the moonlight.

Day 5

"Pan flat, this should be easy," I uttered, tightening the cinches on my laces.

It was 7:00 a.m. and the unobstructed morning sun bore down, but the reflection off the chalk-white lake bed was a new kind of heat . . . a broiler type like nothing I'd felt before.

Despite the heat, I was making good time with a steady pace; my steps were rhythmic and accounted for. I literally counted every single step to break up the monotony of walking so slowly.

I established a reward routine: for every one hundred perfect steps, I got to take a tasty sip of hot water. For every one thousand steps, I earned a ten-minute sit-down rest. I spoke out loud and sang songs to myself. I reflected on fond memories and randomly joked with Dom. My eyes, though, never left the horizon.

In the distance there was a small, dark anomaly atop the glistening plain. A single rock sat with what seemed like a long snail trail behind it, etched into the baked surface. This strange trail revealed its path, but how it made its way into the middle of this dry, desolate lake bed befuddled me. And while standing beside it, I pondered our paths.

I was becoming delirious. Usually while walking I compartmentalized my focus on balance, stepping, counting, and conversing . . . but in a momentary lapse in concentration, it all became jumbled in my head and I stumbled. I collapsed onto the cracked desert floor.

The lone stone lay next to me, only feet away; we were at eye level. And just like the day of my accident, I stared at that stone and recognized our semblance.

Dom rushed over and sat me upright.

"Dammit, dude!" he exclaimed. "Are you all right?"

He helped me up into my chair and placed my feet on the stool.

"Let me check your ankles and knees, mate," he added.

"I lost concentration and caught my right foot," I said. "This desert may seem flat to you, but it's full of cracks and edges that I have to overcome with every step."

Dom flexed my ankle and bent my knee back and forth.

"I think it's time for tape and compression socks."

"I'll limp it home from here!" I joked and stood, ready to continue.

The sun was setting and the twinkling lights of Baker, an aptly named town, were bright in the distance. Our destination was only three miles away. My plan was to walk into the night as far as possible to lessen the final day's effort, as I knew I would be in a lot of pain.

As twilight dwelled around me, my movements became automated; my mind moved beyond thoughts. In a rhythmic, meditative state, I felt myself merge with the mountains and with the omnipresent force of the universe.

As if in an out-of-body experience, I observed objectively the ebb and flow of energy transference in all things in my awareness. My sight was again ones and zeros—I could see behind the veil the basic code of all things without form or boundaries.

I grew tired and Dom was worried. He'd been trying to talk to me for the past thirty minutes. I seemed like a catatonic zombie, unresponsive and marching ever forward. I snapped out of it enough to reassure him that I was alright and ready to end the day.

Day 6

How uncomfortable are you willing to get? I asked myself while waking that final day.

Ambiguous pain radiated through my entire body as I sat up in my sleeping bag.

"I slept terribly," I mumbled, reaching for my coffee mug.

"You've only got two miles to go until you hit the tarmac of the Baker Airport runway," Dom rallied.

There was no relaxing coffee chat, breakfast reflections, or music to start the day; it was pure business . . . get to the end. The smooth lake bed gave way to an undulating quarry of rock and bush—a technical surface for me to navigate, especially when tired. Again, I fixated on the horizon and stared far beyond Baker as shapes and color blended together into a watercolor kaleidoscope.

After a half day's walk, and with only a half mile to go, a curious movement caught my eye—a dark shape slowly zigged and zagged among rolling tumbleweeds. With each step the mirage figure grew, seemingly coming toward me.

The late-afternoon sun caught her sunglasses and refracted a beam of light at me; I could make out her hair flowing in the heat. My heart swelled and my throat tightened when I realized that it was my love, Katie, coming to meet me.

I collapsed onto her shoulder and, out of nowhere, a flood of emotion overcame me. I broke down and cried more deeply than I can ever remember crying.

In that mesmeric moment, I stood on my once-paralyzed feet. I'd just walked more than twenty miles across Death Valley and into the arms of my fiancée. I felt like I had come full circle. I had faced my adversity and risen above it, on my terms.

I bowed my head and said, "I am not what happened to me. I am who I choose to become . . . the Weaver."

With Katie's hand in mine, we slowly pushed the buggy together for the final few hundred feet. At the same time we stepped onto the blacktop runway, where my black van awaited.

I yelled out to the desert behind me and kissed the air, "THANK YOU!"

The Big Picture

Eighty-seven thousand steps, give or take a few, led me to the altar—a sacred place where Katie and I met to commit ourselves in front of our closest friends and family.

In a thick Cuban accent, I parodied Tony Montana, "I like her the first time I laid eyes on her, I think—she's a tiger; she belong to me," I said midvows.

Most of the attendees erupted in laughter—my side of the family, mostly. Her side, crickets; they didn't quite understand my joke. I mischievously winked and nodded at my mother-in-law to acknowledge that it was just a lighthearted joke and carried on.

Katie and I kissed and again, her hand in mine, we walked down the aisle toward our future.

We celebrated on a hilltop in the Malibu mountains under a full moon with one hundred of our closest family members and friends looking on.

I slowly dipped and twirled my new bride on the dance floor, careful not to flub up our practiced choreography. Our song faded out, and whistles, claps, hoots, and hollers rang out as I dipped Katie one last time . . . the signal to our DJ to turn up the beat.

The dance floor immediately flooded with shoeless bridesmaids and drink-wielding groomsmen ready to get their groove on. My quirky aunt Ted grabbed the mic stand from the DJ and began to lip-synch the song "No Diggity," her hips shaking and a finger taunting the crowd. My cousins and I teared up from laughter and sang loudly along with her.

The soft glow of the low-strung market lights lit the faces of all my favorite people, sparking an overwhelming emotion I'd never felt. I returned to my seat, sat behind my slice of wedding cake, and cried. I was grateful for it all. For the pain and the suffering, for the joys and the triumphs, and for every single teeny tiny step I'd taken to get to this point. I was grateful.

Our storybook wedding night ended with Katie and me sitting on a hotel room floor surrounded by a handful of friends.

"Pass the barbecue sauce!" I slurred as I dipped and stuffed my face with another Chicken McNugget.

Still in her gown, Katie laughed and rolled on the ground . . . her bare feet dirtied from the dance floor.

"I can't believe we're eating McDonald's on our wedding night!" she cackled, sipping her Coke and then swiping a fry through the ketchup.

"What a night!" we wailed.

The Stroke of a Pen

"The world is a wheel. When we rise or fall,
we do it together."

Toots, Katie, and I sat around the kitchen table, anxious, frustrated, and scared about the life-changing decision we were about to make. Our business partnership with Taylor at C.O.R.E. had deteriorated due to a difference in visions we had for the company, and we knew it was time for a big change. Our proverbial baby, the business Toots and I had raised out of the ashes of my injury and given every last ounce of energy to, was now up for adoption.

We'd contemplated every possible scenario—consulted with our family and friends, business confidants, and legal counsel. Aside from my injury itself, this was the most challenging decision of our lives.

We'd transformed our personal trauma and transcended its pain by being in service to others. Closing the doors of C.O.R.E. was not an option in our minds.

"It's too damn important!" I exclaimed, pounding my fist on the table. "We know firsthand how much the community needs a place like this, and how important ongoing exercise is for a person's quality of life."

We struggled for months with what we should do. It really wasn't until the eleventh hour that my friend Jared sparked an "aha" moment that completely changed my mind.

As I told him the dilemma we were in, he quickly and genuinely replied: "Congratulations! You're selling your first business."

I hadn't heard our circumstances framed in that context before. It was an epiphany! In that instant I shifted 180 degrees to an empowered state of mind.

"We did create something good, didn't we?" I said. "Wow! Thank you, Jared. I actually feel really good about it now."

What is the cliché? **"If you love something, let it go."** That statement was no truer than in that moment.

Behind closed doors, Toots and I sat beside each other quietly with pens in hand. With a single stroke, we wrote our final chapter of C.O.R.E. and sold our majority share of the business to Taylor. We knew that he would continue to treat the clients in that location for the rest of his life, and we were happy knowing that. We also knew that our best times and the best work the three of us had done together were behind us. I will always honor those memories and the good times we had, but it was now time to move forward.

As the office's building doors opened in front of us, a new world-view came into focus. I felt liberated, stared into the sky, and imagined the perspective lines of a long road with no end converging at the horizon. A sense of hope for my future filled me. Although I had no idea what I would do next, my mind was open to the pure possibility.

What pleased me the most, though—seeing Toots retire from the everyday grind. She had sacrificed so many of her personal dreams for me and my recovery, and she risked every dime on a long-shot start-up business. She gave all her time and energy to me and the community we served, and it was high time for her to enjoy life . . . on her terms.

She leaned into life as a grandmother to Arielle's two young boys, James and Mason, and traveled abroad through Europe. She and her life partner, Hans, met Katie and me on a rainy street corner in Vienna, Austria, where we galivanted over cobblestone, among castles and courtyards. We toasted steins of Weissbier in Munich, Germany, and sipped espressos on the shoreline of lake Lago di Garda, Italy. Her world was opening up again, and she welcomed it all with open arms. This made me happy.

A New Chapter

The year 2020 was one for the history books. Just months after the sale of C.O.R.E., my busy schedule of consulting, public speaking, and my new fitness pursuit, stair-climbing: climbing one step at a time up thousands of stairs in the stairwells of some of the tallest skyscrapers in the country—ground to a screeching halt. A coronavirus called COVID-19 swept the globe and paralyzed most of the world's economy and psyche. The impact of mandatory shutdowns severely impacted not only me and my family, but also countless other families, businesses, and communities around the world.

Katie and I attempted to pivot our business like so many others did, but we struggled to stay ahead. In addition to the never-ending demands of my injury, I felt pressured to provide stability for us. We were locked down, quarantined for months.

The struggle felt oddly familiar, though; it was similar to the early days of my recovery, where I was isolated from the world I once knew. The roller coaster of tormented thoughts and emotions set in.

"Get back to the **B.A.S.I.C.S**, Baker!" I encouraged myself in the mirror. "Baby steps! Just like recovery."

I circled back to the beginning and focused on my breath, then turned my awareness inward. Each day I began with a mantra for a calm mind: Gratitude.

I surrendered to the circumstances that were out of my control and reframed, then refocused, on the things that I could control and paid homage to the present moment with a prayer: "I love you, body. Thank you. Thank you for my awareness and strength. Thank you for the energy that flows to and through me, and for the love and health of my family and friends. I am grateful."

I became inspired as Katie and I continued our commitment—a

healthy routine of exercise, outdoor activities, and nutritious foods. We'd stockpiled tons of frozen homemade meals, emergency items, and, yes, toilet paper.

I, like so many, plugged into the internet and began working via Zoom conferences—a way to continue sharing my experience and knowledge.

We implored a basic system of choices that became healthy habits, very similar to the lifestyle I'd led with Toots for much of my recovery. It was a simple and repeatable approach that we could live by consistently over time . . . the same design that had allowed me to achieve many of my recovery goals . . . the **B.A.S.I.C.S.**

"Success is a staircase of daily steps."

While working on our computers one ordinary afternoon, Katie disappeared for a moment. A few minutes later, she returned unassumingly and continued to work.

"Is everything OK?" I asked.

"Yeah," she replied. "I just took a test. I'm pregnant."

I stopped typing and stared at her. We both grinned but held back our excitement. We'd been down this road before. Katie had suffered two painful miscarriages, which took a toll on her body and mind.

We'd romanticized starting a family but knew that the odds were against us. The first time Katie became pregnant we were over the moon! We didn't hold back our excitement and shared the news early with family and friends, only to be devastated a couple of weeks later when Katie began to bleed. The doctor confirmed there was no heartbeat.

The second time, after receiving the news that Katie's blood levels showed a viable pregnancy, she was shopping at the market when a familiar feeling came over her. She left her basket full of items in the produce aisle and went to the bathroom, only to see blood again.

Katie called me while I was at work, and I quickly rushed to meet her at the ER. We held out hope, knowing that bleeding can happen in the early stages of a pregnancy, but once again we were met with the devastating news that there was no heartbeat.

Gun shy from our past experiences, we knew not to get overjoyed too soon and to keep the news private.

I still felt a bit reluctant, fearful of my ability to be a father with a spinal cord injury.

"How can I handle a child when I myself am a big baby?" I'd confided to Toots a few years back after a bike ride. "My injury takes a lot of time, energy, attention, and resources."

Katie and I carried on despite the fear and uncertainty. We sold our house in Santa Clarita and moved into a dream home on a hill. We tucked ourselves away in our new little nest and prepared for our next chapter, the third time being the charm.

Full Circle

"All that we are is the result of what we have thought."
—BUDDHA

As I sat poolside in the corner of our yard, the late-summer sun warmed my neck. I gazed over the San Fernando Valley from atop the hill.

I turned and caught my reflection in the crystal-blue water and remembered my once tear-stained face staring back. It seemed like a lifetime ago when I'd sat at the water's edge, contemplating suicide.

I looked deeper into the water and thought; I understood that boy and his pain. He still lives in me today.

The weight of the world, gravity, responsibility, and aging with a spinal cord injury is heavy and hard to carry. I still struggle day to day. I've slowed a bit in recent years . . . but just enough to smell the roses.

I thought of the darkness and the depths of suffering I'd endured and recounted the processes I'd implored.

"It's been one hell of a ride," I said to myself as I stared at the ripple in the water.

The translucent waves began to smooth as a new reflection gleamed. A tiny finger dipped in the water. I looked again; it was no longer just me I saw—it was my daughter.

I have often said that "I would not change a thing," and it is true. I am grateful and I have never been happier in my entire life than I am right now!

The moment Cayla Mae Baker was placed in my arms I looked into her tiny eyes and saw the raw wonder of the world and the unobstructed love that conquers all. Her gaze held the infinite and reminded me that I had come full circle. My spinal cord injury that for so long monopolized my everyday life seemed to no longer matter. She looked at me and I knew, right then, that my adversity had prepared me for that moment. I was now a father—responsible for the love and care of this beautiful life—to provide, guide, and protect, injury or not. An overwhelming sense of strength, on a cellular level, seemed to be activated, switched on, as though I was literally made for this. My paternal instincts took over and I became emboldened.

My little family and I live a simple yet full, peaceful life, and I can say, honestly, that the ride was worth it!

Life, by its very nature, is cyclical; it is a recurring cycle of events; the good, the bad, the difficult, and the indifferent are all ongoing and indefinite. These experiences can bear great fruit if seen through the lens of optimism and opportunity.

I feel the quality of my life has been enhanced in immeasurable ways, and I am deeply obliged to the many people who have loved, supported, and guided me along the way. It has been through adversity that the depth and breadth of my perspective has been cultivated, of which, today, I value most.

And every day I get to remind myself that I am the weaver. The basic choices, routines, and habits that I form are within my control. My thoughts, words, and actions are an artistic expression of my will.

"I am the master of my fate:
I am the captain of my soul."
—W. E. HENLEY

I move through life like a rock climber without ropes. Every slow, thoughtful movement advances me forward and up. I cannot afford to slip. There is no wasted movement, no wasted energy.

In the process I have become a student of my own suffering and have honed a method for a grateful heart, a resilient mind, an emboldened body, and a gracious lifestyle. I used my fear as fuel and anger for amplitude.

"I am not what happened to me,
I am who I choose to become."
—CARL JUNG

I discovered my purpose in death—to share my time and love. And I found my passion in life—to teach and guide others out of the dark and into the light. It is a reciprocal transference of human energy and inspiration . . . a mirror—a reflective connection to myself and to you.

We are all on a heroic journey with stories worth telling and achievements worth applauding. My mission is to help you think and move your way through adversity with a basic cycle of mind, body, spirit, and lifestyle choices to discover peace, power, joy, and reverence for life.

May my story activate something primal inside of you—a desire to rise above challenge and become the highest version of yourself and to live in that space, gracefully.

My maxim:

"Hold the Vision, Do the Work, Trust the Process."

The adversity *is* the adventure!

As Neo postulated in the final scene of the movie *The Matrix*:

"I didn't come here to tell you how this is going to end. I came here to tell you how it's going to begin.... A world without rules and controls, without borders and boundaries. A world where anything is possible. Where we go from there is a choice I leave to you."

This is the Rebellious Recovery.

TO MY YOUNGER SELF

Purpose found me the moment I availed my heart, opened my mind, and began sharing my life with others. My vulnerability is my strength and gives others permission to relate and share with me an authentic connection. I am no longer alone in my insecurity. By serving others from this pure space, magic happens. A transcendence occurs—a transformation from me to we.

In the end, all we have is time and love, and all we can do is *share*.

Scan the QR code and head to therebelliousrecovery.com/serve-%26-share for this part's complementary photo gallery.

WINGS FOR LIFE

The future is forged by those willing to explore beyond boundaries, to risk and face failure for the discovery of something new, profound and meaningful. They are the bold and the brave that despite odds, persist and ask the questions "*If not us, who?*" "*If not now, when?*." Their long-view gives us hope for a brighter tomorrow and the confidence that we, as humanity, are being cared for.

Wings for Life is a not-for-profit spinal cord research foundation. Their mission is to find a cure for spinal cord injury. They fund world-class scientific research and clinical trials around the globe aimed at healing the injured spinal cord.

For more information visit www.wingsforlife.com

I am a proud Wings For Life ambassador and a passionate member of the board of directors, USA. I work with an extraordinary team of doctors, scientists, researchers and philanthropists from around the world that seek to discover solutions to spinal cord injury. I have dedicated my life and a portion of the profits from this book to the legacy of Wings For Life. Together, we rise by lifting others.

ACKNOWLEDGMENTS

I dedicate this book to my daughter, Cayla Mae Baker.

Sweetheart, life is a grand adventure! No matter the challenges we face, our time on earth can be filled with sunlit peaks and moonless valleys—it's a vast, magical spectrum of experience.

I learned that the two most important notions in life are time and love, and all we can do with them is share them. Share love with your whole heart. Be gracious yet discerning with your time, and give reverence for all things. And remember, a single loving flame can light a dark world afire!

The only difference between you and the happiest person in the world is the six inches between your ears . . . it's all in your mind, sweetheart. You can do anything!

May my story remind you.

I love you, Dad.

I think of my life as an Adventures of . . . type of tale imbued with great teachings and many bright souls, guides, and mentors along my wild and woolly journey. I bow my head with thanks for my family members and friends who've enhanced my life with color. You've helped me create a mosaic life—diverse, dimensional, fulfilled, and revered.

I have many people to thank.

I'll begin with my Toots. I truly am here today because of my mother, Laquita Dian, my "Toots." Without you, I would have been gone long ago. You raised me, saved me, and sent me on to soar. Your fierce, unconditional love is the example I wish to pay forward to my daughter. My simple words alone cannot convey my gratitude, my thankfulness, and my deepest heartfelt love for you. All I can say is thank you. I love you.

To my wife, Katelyn. You found me at a divine time when I least expected it. Our paths crossed and I immediately fell for your radiant love—it transcended my struggles. You saw beyond my injury and into my heart and chose to share your life with me, one which you knew would be a challenge. Thank you for being my partner, my best friend, my critic, and my counterbalance in life. I honor and love you with all my heart, and as I said before in our vows:

"My entire life has culminated to this point, in this moment, where I stand with honor and with immense gratitude to be here in your divine radiance. From the moment I laid eyes on you, I thought to myself, 'She's a tiger.'

I had never before seen anyone carry themselves the way that you do. It's the way you smile, the way you laugh, and the way your light illuminates a room. It's that light that has been a beacon for my heart. You are all I have ever imagined in a partner. Your love, and the way you share your love, inspires me to be the highest version of myself for you. May I always be your mirror, to reflect to you, all the beauty and all the goodness you give me. I am so excited to begin this new chapter of our lives together . . . to travel and taste the world together. To create and build our dreams. And to one day add to our beautiful family.

Katie, I honor you, respect you, and admire all that you are. With all that I am . . . I love you."

Thank you, Dad (Daniel G.), for your enduring love and support. You've always believed in me. You helped raise my boyhood dreams and buoyed me in my most desperate hours. You paved a way for me to seek more in life and showed me how to share . . . and the importance of sniffing flowers.

Arielle, my sister. You have always been like a brother to me. We frolicked and fought as adolescents and endured childhood traumas together. We'd lean on each other, share our friends, and explore the limits of our nature. I love you and hold the utmost respect for your strength of character and admire the life you've built for yourself and your boys, James Michael Aaron and Mason Michelangelo. Thank you for always being there.

To the matriarchs and patriarchs of my mother's family: my great-grandparents Anna and Oakland Keith Irwin and my beloved grandparents Mimi (Barbara Ann) and Papa (Kenneth Stovall). Y'all taught me what it means to be as tough as old boot leather, to love with my whole heart, and to be as tenacious as a badger. You've come from a long bloodline of Cherokee Indians, Norwegian immigrants, and German settlers; our ancestry is honored and alive and well in me. I love you.

And to the rest of my kinfolk: my aunts Julie, Neta, Sonja, Gwenny, and Suzy . . . and the boys: Te, Bowdy, Josh, Jeremy, Scott, Sheldon, Boyce, Heath, Aaron, and our lovely Emmerson. And my uncles Jack, Chuck, Carl, Kenny, Keith, Kevin, Joey, and Rick (a.k.a. Uncle Vito) . . . thank you, too, I love you.

To my father's family: Grandma B and Grampa Ed, I'll always love and cherish your memory. I hold you close to my heart and even closer to my stomach anytime I eat perogies! My aunts Leslie and Wendy, Uncle Joe, and the kids: Lance and Jennifer. I love you.

And my extended family: my mother-in-law, Carol; my father-in-law, Frank; and my sister-in-law, Meghan, and her husband, Jared. I love you all, and I'm so grateful to have been so warmly welcomed into your BIG loving family!

And to my dearest friends, you are the family that I choose: Lynn Lupetti and Ed Lohmann, you both have loved, encouraged, and supported me in the most adoring way. I feel so lucky to have you in my life. Thank you. I love you.

Adam Zerbe, my oldest friend. I love you. Thank you for all you've done for me and my family. We can always pick right up where we've left off, no matter the chasm of time. Your cheeky laugh transports me back to some of my earliest memories and into the bowl of Cheerios we used to share.

Adam Bice, I've always admired you. Your easy going Malibu vibe mashed up with a quick wit, common sense, and physical prowess is the combo I was drawn to all those years ago. Thank you for always having my back and saying YES to my shenanigans.

Marc Jolley . . . our friendship endures, brother. Your queries into my life after all these years keep our foundation strong. Thank you.

Josh Baltimore, you are a steadfast rock! You've never wavered as a friend. When I think about loyalty, I think about you. No questions asked, you've always been there! Thank you.

To so many more past and present friends: Mitchell Sanchez, Christopher Voelker, Billy Dias, Tara Llanes, Brian & Lisa Cernius, Matt Armstrong, Luke Wilson, Sam Morris, Andy Bray, Josh Chisum, Donovan Mitchell, Todd Hicks, Dave Crook, Ben Marius, Troy Becker, Austin, Thomas, Jill and Jimmy Prock, Brandon Jenner, Josh Hansen, Scott Gadburry, Hollyn Thompson, Dominic Gill, Tim Crane, Jared Hillman, Jake Martin, Leon Bostick, Chris Spilfogal, Michael Stahl, Stephanie Minafra, Seth Rosenzweig, Jordan Wilhelm, Brianna Walker, Dave Hurley, and . . . I could go on and on. You all light my life. Thank you!

To my invaluable mentors who have shaped me into the man I am: Hans Stangl, JR Canaguier, Jan & Rick Babington, Taylor Isaacs, Peterson Conway, and Jim Snell. I have absorbed so many vital lessons from each and every one of you. My life and mindset is literally an amalgamation of the knowledge and wisdom you've shared. My sincerest gratitude and thanks to you all.

And finally, to my publishing team: I am the sum of my sphere, the tip of the spear—the aggregate of a small handful of artists and wordsmiths that I owe a debt of gratitude. My thoughts and words were shaped, guided, and distilled artfully by you, so thank you.

To Sam Maddox, I appreciate you always being a text or phone call away. Above all else, I regard you as a sage, an enigmatic mage and deep contemplator—a true curiositor. Your insights helped shape the spine of my book (pun intended) and the underlying messaging I intended to share. Thank you.

Stephanie Mojica, my content editor, you wielded your wand, a scalpel of sorts, across my first and second drafts to craft my story in a way my work alone could not convey. Thank you for building the foundation—everything henceforth was built off your magic.

James Gallagher, my copy editor, thank you! You are the bow on this gift I am so proud to share.

Kory Kirby, you are a kindred spirit and a craftsmen through and through. My search for the perfect publishing partner, book designer, and literary guide led me to your inbox—the place where our paths crossed and the road opened. Cheers to you, my friend. We have many good miles ahead!

Adam Bice, my brother from another mother, thank you for creating the cover of this book. You perfectly illustrated my vision and captured the essence of this story . . . one you know so well. It means the world to me.

Thank you, Chris Boulton, for your sublime art. Your photograph tells a thousand words.

"Together we rise!"

ABOUT THE AUTHOR

"Lying there in the dirt, motionless and completely aware of my plight, brought forth a life-altering realization of my place in life. No longer being a professional motorcycle rider, skateboarder, surfer, snowboarder, mountain biker, or even a simple fisher made me realize that I am destined to do far greater things in my life than win championships aboard a motorcycle. Things that affect people's lives. I can help people through my own adversity, bringing hope and inspiration to those without."

Aaron Baker, former professional motocross athlete, sustained a career-ending spinal cord injury in 1999. He fractured cervical vertebrae 4, 5, and 6 in his neck, rendering him quadriplegic.

From the onset of his injury, his focus was on maximizing his quality of life through consistent, long-term restorative exercise. Throughout his process of recovery, Aaron has been credited with numerous world firsts, including two cross-country cycling tours, multiple cycling national championship events (with a 2011 Paracycling National Championship title), and two Mammoth Mountain Kamikaze Bike Games adaptive class wins. Additionally, a documentary film *Coming to My Senses*, covering Aaron's twenty-mile solo trek across the infamous Death Valley desert in California, was released through Netflix and Amazon.

Aaron is an adventure athlete, author, orator, entrepreneur, and ambassador for spinal cord injury. He cofounded the Center of Restorative Exercise and is a member of the board of directors, USA, and chair of the Ambassador Council for Red Bull's nonprofit Wings for Life Foundation.

Aaron also sits on the board of directors for the Los Angeles based nonprofit Artists for Trauma. He is a spinal cord injury lifestyle specialist and author for multiple blue chip organizations and a contributor for the *Huffington Post*.

Timeline of Events and Milestones

"My process of recovery and redefinition has only been realized by a collective effort of full commitment. Without support and effort from my family and friends, none of the achievements would have been realized, nor would my current state of ability and health be possible."

1995: Amateur Motocross Athlete
- Motocross Amateur National Champion at Loretta Lynn's
- Grand National Champion in Ponca City
- Youth World Champion

1998: Professional Motocross Athlete
- Signed professional contract with Suzuki

1999: Spinal Cord Injury and Respiratory Failure
- C4, C5, and C6 initially diagnosed as a complete injury

- Lungs filled with fluid (pneumonia), suffocated and flatlined for one minute

Recovery:

For the first four years of his recovery process, Aaron was completely dependent and needed full assistance with all activities of daily living (e.g., bathing, feeding, dressing, and moving). All subsequent milestones were achieved based on the continued assistance of his mother and full-time caretaker, Laquita.

Tandem Bicycle:

- 2003–2007: LA Marathon
- 2006: Rosarito to Ensenada, Mexico
- 2007: Rise Above Tour cross-country ride from San Diego, California, to St. Augustine, Florida—total of 3,182 miles

Trike Bike:

- 2008: LA Marathon
- 2008: Rise Above Tour cross-country ride from San Francisco, California, to Washington, DC—total of 4,202 miles
- 2009: US Paralympic Training at the Chula Vista Olympic Training Center, California
- 2009–2011: National Time Trial Champion—T1 Trike Category
- 2012: Selected to the National US Paralympic Team for the London Olympic Games

The Center of Restorative Exercise (C.O.R.E.):

- January 1, 2011: Opened the wellness facility in Los Angeles, California

Death Valley Walk:

- October 2013: Walked twenty miles across Death Valley, California
- September 2018: Documentary *Coming to My Senses* released through Netflix and Amazon

Red Bull's Wings for Life World Run:
- 2014–2020: Los Angeles, Miami, and Austria

Off-Road Mountain Bike (The Honey Badger):
- 2014–2016: Won first place in the Adaptive Downhill class at the Kamikaze Bike Games in Mammoth Mountain, California

Skyscraper Stair Climb Events:
- 2019: US Bank Tower, Los Angeles (1,664 stairs)
- 2019: Willis Tower, Chicago (2,109 stairs)

Personal:
- September 2015: Married Katelyn Baker
- July 2019: The sale of C.O.R.E.
- 2020: Started a new company, Baker Active LLC
- December 2020: Welcomed daughter Cayla Mae Baker

Where to find me online

Website: www.imaaronbaker.com
Facebook: www.facebook.com/aaron.baker.9634
Instagram: @imaaronbaker
Twitter: @imaaronbaker
YouTube: www.youtube.com/user/aaronbaker

Printed in Great Britain
by Amazon

30094846R00129